Armin Lindauer
vorWand und entTäuschung



KERBER ART

Es ist schwer auf hellem Grund zu malen und
es ist schwer auf dunklem Grund zu malen,
aber am schwersten ist es, ohne Grund zu malen.

*It is hard to paint on light ground*
*And it is hard to paint on dark ground*
*But hardest of all is to paint with no grounds for doing so.*

**Armin Lindauer**
**vorWand und entTäuschung**

herausgegeben von/*published by*
Martin Stather

**Du sollst Dir kein Bild machen**
22. – 28. September 2014
POT 72 Artspace, Berlin
kuratiert von Eleonora Frolov

**vorWand und entTäuschung**
13. November 2014 – 29. Januar 2015
Mannheimer Kunstverein
kuratiert von Martin Starter

**Gebetsteppiche**
9. September – 9. Oktober 2016
St. Christophorus, Berlin
kuratiert von Celia Caturelli
in Zusammenarbeit mit Eleonora Frolov

**Ein Bild ist kein Bild ist ein Bild**
10. September – 1. Oktober 2016
Galerie Z, Berlin
kuratiert von Eleonora Frolov

***You shall not make for yourself an image***
*September, 22th – 28th 2014*
*POT 72 Artspace, Berlin*
*curated by Eleonora Frolov*

***Pretext and disappointment***
*November, 13th 2014 – January, 29th 2015*
*Mannheimer Kunstverein*
*curated by Martin Starter*

***Prayer Rugs***
*September, 9th – October, 9th 2016*
*St. Christophorus, Berlin*
*curated by Celia Caturelli*
*in cooperation with Eleonora Frolov*

***A picture is no picture is a picture***
*September, 10th – October, 1st 2016*
*Galerie Z, Berlin*
*curated by Eleonora Frolov*

**Inhalt**



***Content***

# Ein Bild ist kein Bild ist ein Bild

**Martin Stather //** Kunsthistoriker und
künstlerischer Leiter / Kurator des Kunstvereins Mannheim

**»Ceci n´est pas une pipe.«** René Magritte

Armin Lindauer geht mit offenen Augen durch die Welt und dort im Besonderen durch Galerien und Museen. Offenbar fühlt er sich genötigt, mit seiner Kunst darauf zu reagieren, konzeptuell darauf zu antworten und sich als Quertreiber zu betätigen. Nun sind Künstler per se notorische Unruhestifter, was nicht weiter verwundern sollte, denn schließlich ist gerade auch das ihre Aufgabe. Lindauer jedoch stiftet, nach genauer Beobachtung, sehr gezielt Unruhe, beispielsweise schon bei der Präsentation von Kunstwerken und da insbesondere, bei der Rahmung. Genau genommen beginnt das Unruhestiften aber schon früher, nämlich beim Malakt selbst. Dieser wird analysiert, seziert und sodann al Gusto und Gutdünken auf die eine oder andere Weise ausgeführt. Was lässt sich über sein Verhältnis zur Malerei sagen, liebt er oder hasst er sie oder ist es nur große Skepsis mit der er sie betrachtet. Was kann man auch heute noch malen, wo alles bereits gemalt ist, wo alle Stile bis zum Überdruss dekliniert sind, von akribisch bis willenlos, da geht kein Haar mehr dazwischen. In der Konsequenz von Lindauer wird das Bild dekonstruiert, um einen wie auch immer gearteten Neuanfang zu versuchen. Einmal wird der Rahmen selbst zum Bild, zum Inhalt. Bild und Ramen, in der Regel untrennbar verbunden, werden hier getrennt, und was eigentlich zusammengehört wird auf ziemlich perfide Art und Weise dann doch wieder zusammen gefügt, da wird der Rahmen zum Bild und das Bild zum Rahmen seiner selbst wird. Da gibt es Rahmenteile, die sich im Bild wie Systemelemente in Mondrians Bildern konstruktiv neu ordnen, allerdings ohne zu einer schlüssigen Konstruktion zu finden, die sie höchstens als Vorschlag andeuten. Ein anderes mal gibt es Materialbilder mit realen Rahmen, die ins Bild gesetzt sind, entweder in eine Leinwand mit Malspuren oder wiederum innerhalb eines gemalten Rahmens. »Ceci n´est pas un cadre!« würde Magritte solches betiteln, denn: ist ein Rahmen ein Rahmen ein Rahmen? Franz Marc wurde einmal gefragt, warum er denn blaue Pferde male. Er soll geantwortet haben: »Ich male keine blauen Pferde, ich male Bilder.«

**»Do I smell, I smell home cooking. It´s only the river, it´s only the river!«**
Talking Heads

Armin Lindauer ist ein Fallensteller, der den Betrachter mal in die Irre führt, mal mit expressivem Vortrag verführt um ihn zu ent – täuschen. Denkzeichen wie diese zeichnen seine Kunst aus. Das Bild wird stets von Neuem befragt, auseinandergenommen, neu zusammengesetzt. Malweisen, Malstile und Farbauftrag variieren, eine bewusste Wahl wird getroffen und damit schon wieder fragwürdig. Bei dieser Malerei gibt es keine Sicherheit, kein genüssliches Zurücksinken und Genießen –

der Betrachter muss immer auf der Hut sein, sonst geht er dem Künstler ins Netz. Auch die Stofflichkeit seiner Motive wird befragt. Gemalter Stoff wird realem Stoff gegenübergestellt, wie reale Rahmen in gemalte Rahmen gestellt werden. Wo beginnt das Bild, wo hört es auf? Setzt sich das Bild im Raum fort, wenn es an der Wand hängt? In der Regel bestimmen Bilder ihr Umfeld und hören eben nicht am Rahmen auf. Bilder im Bild: Lindauer führt uns in ein Spiegelkabinett, in dem das Spiegelbild des Spiegelbilds des Spiegelbilds zu sehen ist und schon fällt man ins Bodenlose. Was auf der Netzhaut bleibt, ist ein Bild, aber welches eigentlich? Nichts ist, wie es scheint und auch der Schein ist möglicherweise nur ein dürftiger Abglanz, der langsam verschwindet, wie bei der Cheshire-Katze in Alice im Wunderland, deren Grinsen noch anhält, auch wenn die Katze selbst längst verschwunden ist. Kontrolle und Intuition werden auf den Prüfstand gestellt, die industrielle Verbindlichkeit von Farbwerten der Malerei in der Kodak Color Control – Serie gegenübergestellt. Kleine, klassisch anmutende Landschaften werden da in Serie produziert, die sich dennoch mit Leichtigkeit der Farbkontrolle entziehen. Doch damit nicht genug, ein eigenes, kunstimmanentes Kontrollsystem wird etabliert, indem die Farbkontrollstreifen selbst gemalt sind und plötzlich völlig andere Parameter gelten. Das Sich-Entziehen ist eine gut bekannte Strategie in der Kunst, auch schon vor dem 20. Jahrhundert, denn dort gelten andere Regeln als in der Alltagsgesellschaft, die von Normen und deren Beachtung lebt. Kunst darf, sie muss vielleicht anarchisch sein, Undenkbares denken und gestalten, um Veränderung und Erneuerung zu ermöglichen. Hier ist Armin Lindauer unterwegs.

## *A picture is no picture is a picture*

*Martin Stather // art historian and
artistic director/curator at Kunstverein Mannheim*

*»Ceci n'est pas une pipe.«* René Magritte

*Armin Lindauer walks open-eyed through the world and through its galleries and museums in particular. Evidently he feels the need to react to it with his art, to reply to it conceptually, and to act as a troublemaker. Now, artists per se are notorious mischief-makers, which should be no further cause for surprise because, after all, their task is to be precisely that. Lindauer, however, after careful observation, makes trouble very purposely, in the very presentation of artworks for example and in that context, in framing in particular. Strictly speaking, though, the troublemaking starts even sooner, namely during the act of painting itself. This act is analyzed, dissected, and then according to taste and discretion executed in some way or another. What can be said about his relationship to he looks at it? Whatever can one paint these days, when everything has been painted, when all styles have been worked through ad nauseum, from meticulous to slack-willed, there is now barely a hair's breadth between them? With the consistency applied by Lindauer the picture is deconstructed, in order to attempt a new start in whatever form it may be. One time the frame itself becomes the picture, the content. Picture and frame, generally dissociable, are separated here, and what really belongs together is then, quite perfidiously, joined back together after all: the frame becomes the picture and the picture the frame of itself. There are frame sections which – like system elements in Mondrian's pictures – constructively reorder themselves in the picture, but without forming a conclusive construction which they might ultimately hint at. Another time there are material pictures with real frames which are set into the picture, either into a canvas with traces of paint or, again, within a painted frame. »Ceci n'est pas un cadre!« would be how Magritte would title such a thing, for: is a frame a frame a frame? Franz Marc was once asked why he painted blue horses. He is reputed to have replied: »I don't paint blue horses, I paint pictures.«*

*»Do I smell, I smell home cooking. It´s only the river, it's only the river!«* Talking Heads

*Armin Lindauer is a trapper, now leading the beholder astray, now seducing him with expressive talk in order regularly to deceive him, or to disappoint him. Signs of contemplation such as these characterize his art. The picture is constantly re-questioned, taken apart, put together again. Painting methods, painting styles, and color application vary, a conscious choice is made and is thereby, yet again, called into question. With this type of painting there is no certainty, no voluptuous sinking back and enjoying – the beholder must be always on his guard, otherwise he will find himself enmeshed by the artist. The materiality of Lindauer's motifs is also questioned. Painted substance is contrasted with real substance, as real frames are placed in painted frames. Where does the picture start, where does it stop? Does the picture continue in space when it hangs on the wall? Generally, pictures define their surroundings and do not, after all, end at the frame. Pictures within the picture: Lindauer leads us into a hall of mirrors, in which the reflected image of the reflected image of the reflected image can be seen and we are precipitated into a bottomless pit. An image remains on the retina, but which one is it, in fact? Nothing is the way it appears and even appearance is possibly only a paltry reflection that slowly vanishes, as with the Cheshire Cat in Alice in Wonderland, whose grin remains even when the cat itself has long disappeared. Control and intuition are put to the test, the industrial constraint of painting's color values in the Kodak Color Control series juxtaposed. Small, classical-looking landscapes are produced in series here, which nevertheless break free from the color control with ease. This is not all, though: a specific, art-immanent control system is established, in which the color control strips themselves are painted and in which completely different parameters suddenly apply. The breaking away is a well known strategy in art, even before the 20th century, for other rules apply there than in everyday society, which lives on standards and their observance. Art is permitted to be, it needs to be anarchistic, it must conceive of and shape the unthinkable in order to enable change and renewal. Herein lies the task area of Armin Lindauer.*

Manchmal heißt Malen auch,
einen falschen Gedanken
richtig zuende zu denken.
*Sometimes painting means as well*
*bringing a wrong thought*
*to the right close.*

**Diafilmbild / *Positive film picture***
Öl auf Nessel / *Oil on nettle cloth*
135 x 150 cm · 1992

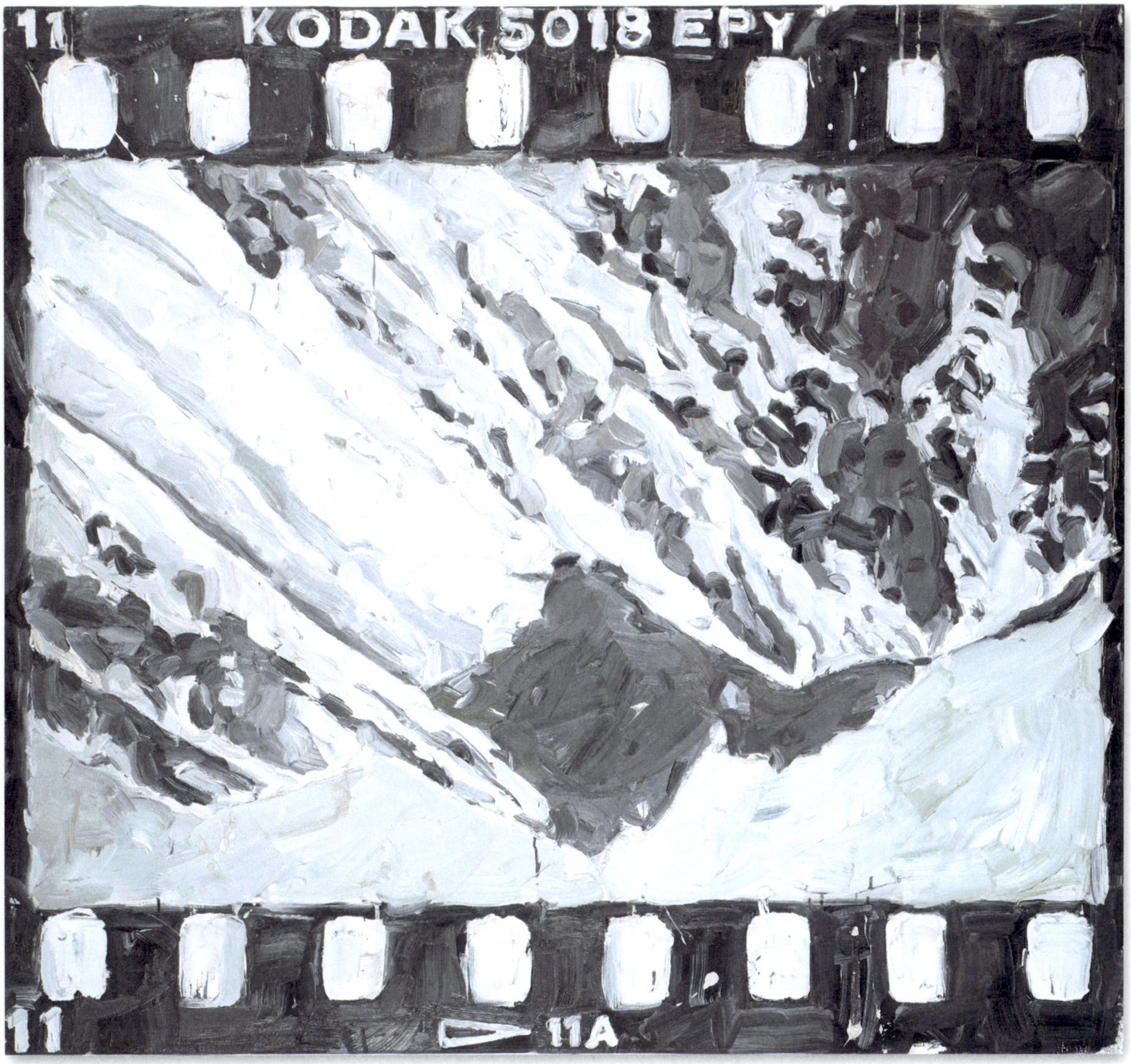
11 KODAK 5018 EPY
11 11A

**Selfcontrol Gray**
links: Acryl und Siebdruck auf Nessel auf Hartfaserplatte
rechts: Öl auf Nessel auf Hartfaserplatte
*left: Acryl and silk screen print on nettle cloth on hardboard*
*right: Oil on nettle cloth on hardboard*
180 x 54 cm je Tafel/*per panel* · 1991

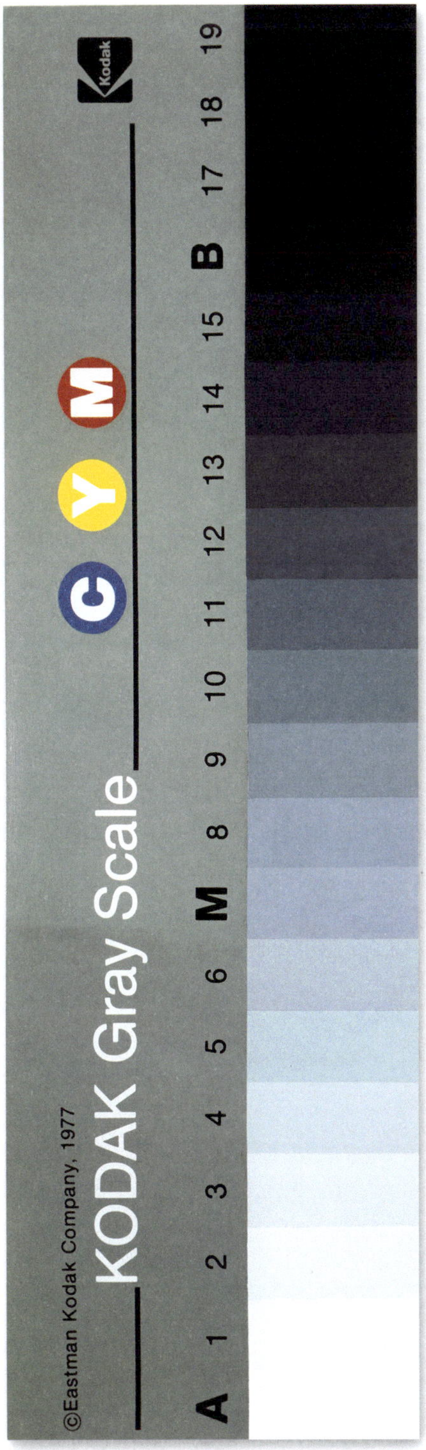
©Eastman Kodak Company, 1977
KODAK Gray Scale
Kodak
C Y M
A 1 2 3 4 5 6 M 8 9 10 11 12 13 14 15 B 17 18 19

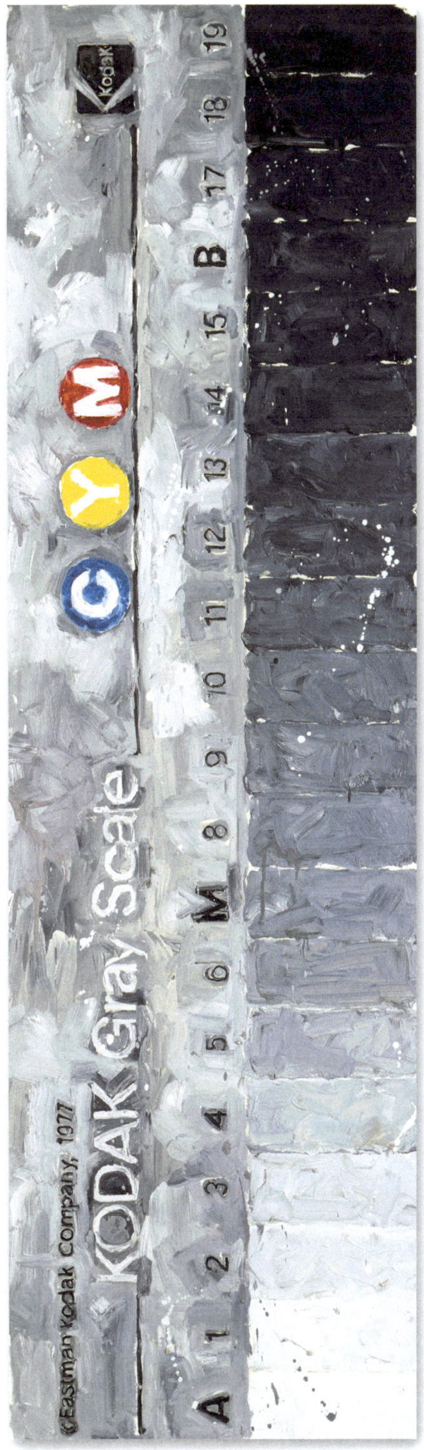
©Eastman Kodak Company, 1977
KODAK Gray Scale
Kodak
C Y M
A 1 2 3 4 5 6 M 8 9 10 11 12 13 14 15 B 17 18 19

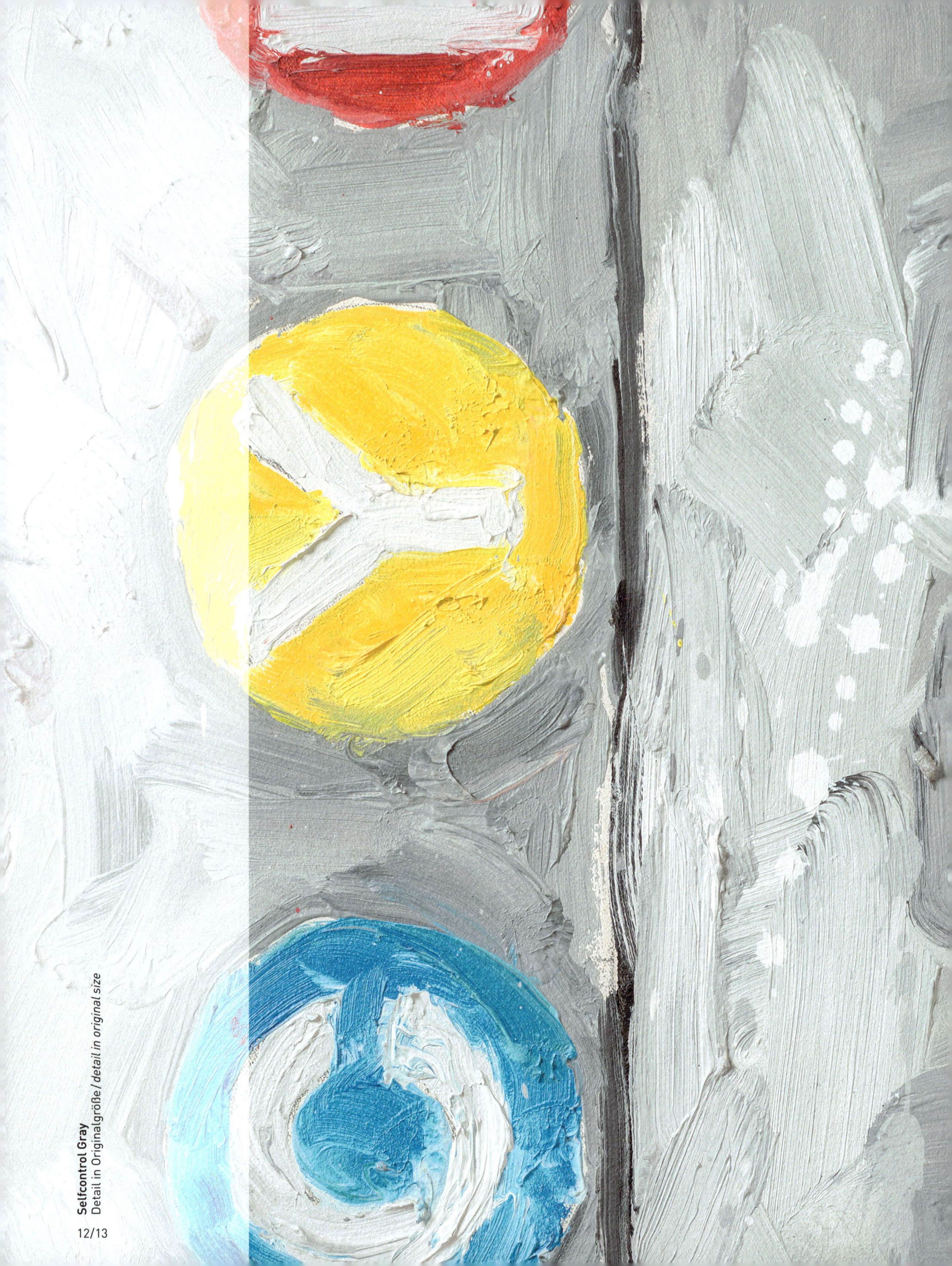

**Selfcontrol Gray**
Detail in Originalgröße / *detail in original size*

13
12

Stets beginne ich mit einem Plan, doch immer entwickelt sich alles anders.
Das heißt nicht, dass man keinen Plan haben sollte oder keinen bräuchte.
Ganz im Gegenteil, ohne Plan ist es furchtbar schwierig anzufangen.
Man muss auch ständig bereit sein, die gemachten Pläne über den Haufen zu werfen,
denn möglicherweise gelingt von den zahllosen Plänen nur der Letzte,
aber auch da gibt es keine Sicherheit.

*I always start with a plan, but everything always turns out differently.
That does not mean that one should not have a plan or does not need one.
On the contrary, without a plan it is terribly difficult to begin.
One also has to be constantly willing to throw over the made plans,
because possibly, of the countless plans, only the final one will succeed,
but even there, there is no certainty.*

**Kodakplanfilm / *Kodak sheet film***
Öl auf Nessel / *Oil on nettle cloth*
126,5 x 160 cm · 1992

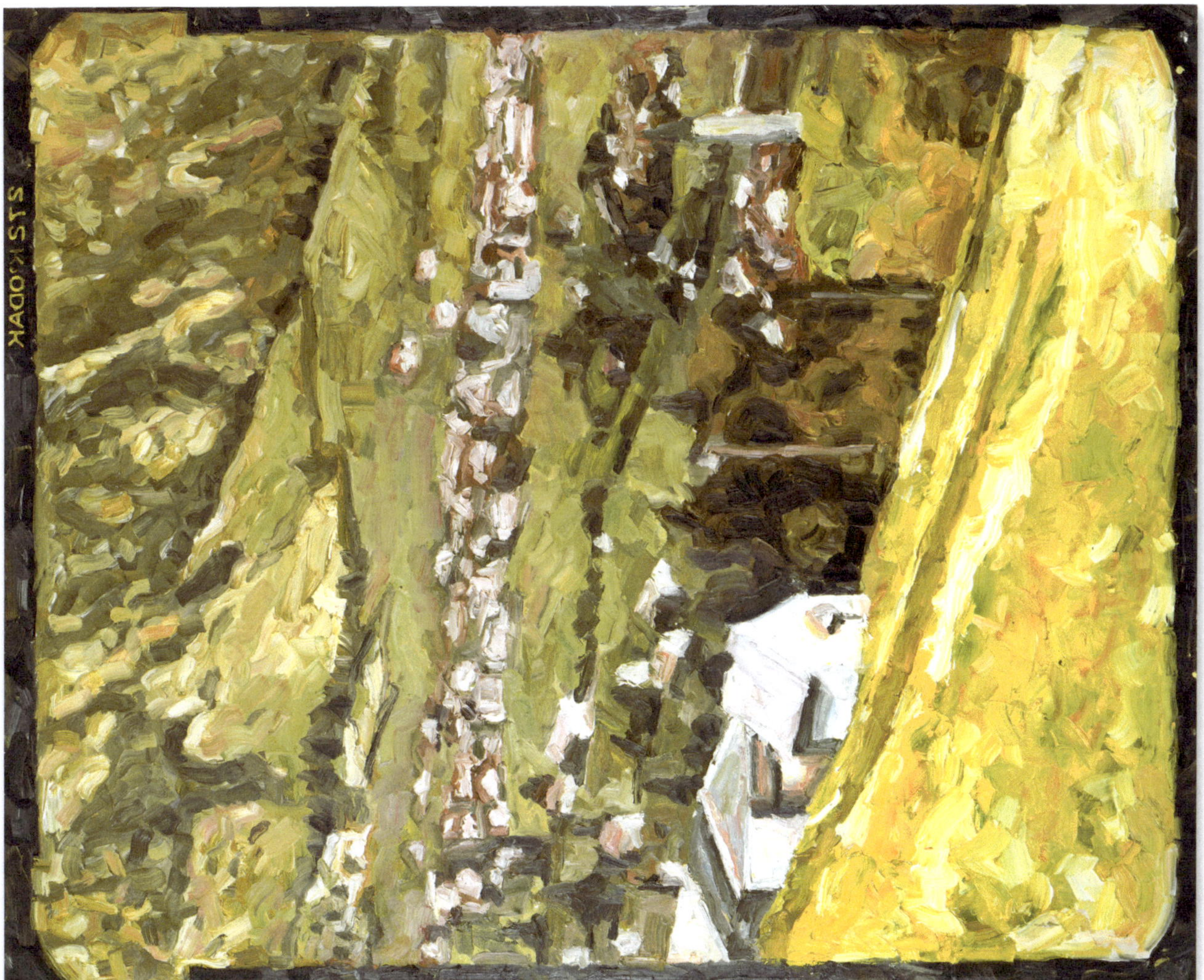
272 KODAK

**Testbild / *Test picture***
Öl auf Sperrholz / *Oil on plywood*
47 x 55 cm · 1992

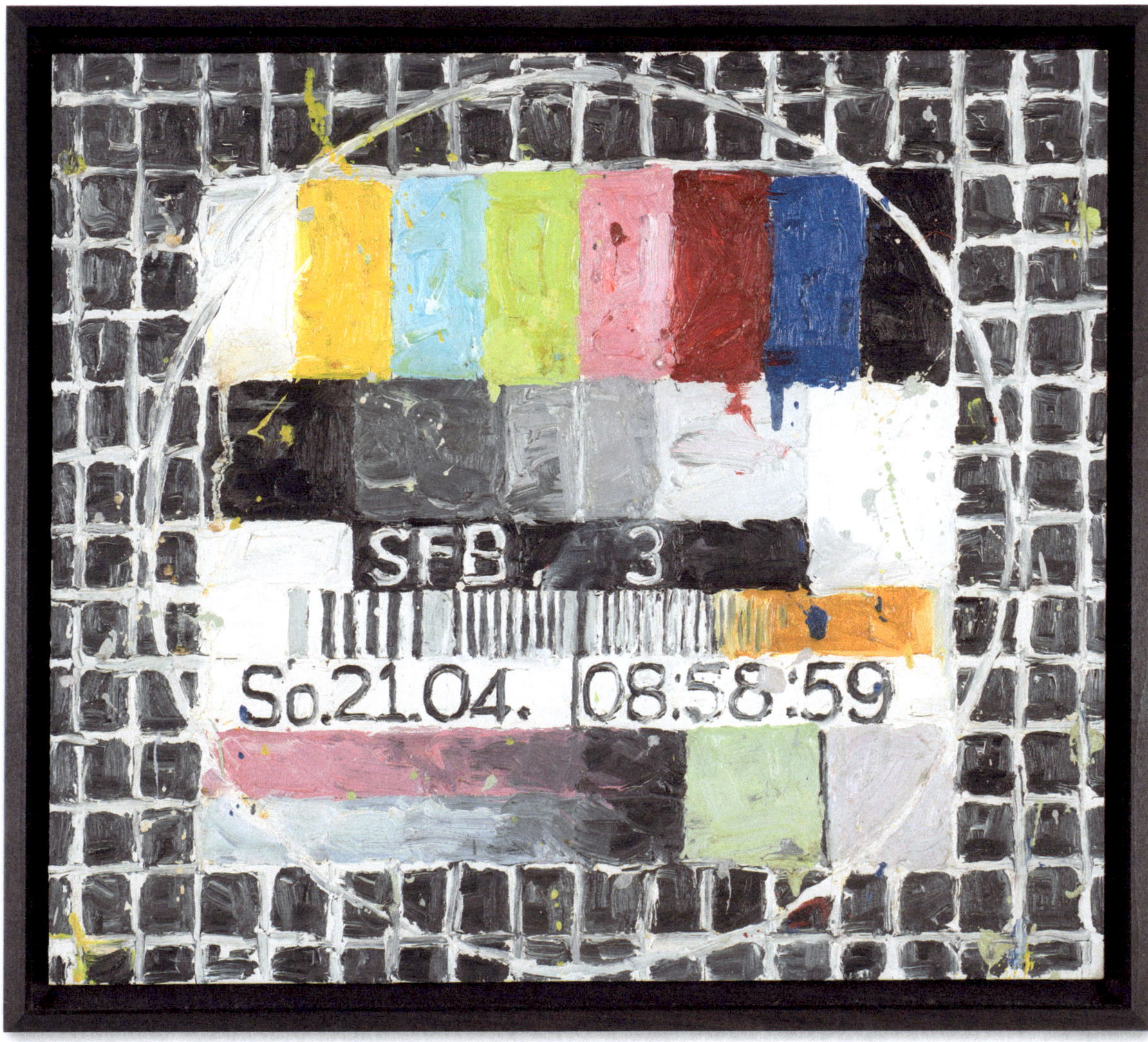
SFB 3
So.21.04. 08:58:59

Stabilität und Sicherheit bieten bloß Erwartetes.
Nur Instabilität und Chaos erzeugen Neues.
*Stability and certainty merely offer the expected.*
*Only instability and chaos produce something new.*

**Testbild / *Test picture***
Öl auf Sperrholz / *Oil on plywood*
42,8 x 48,8 cm · 1992

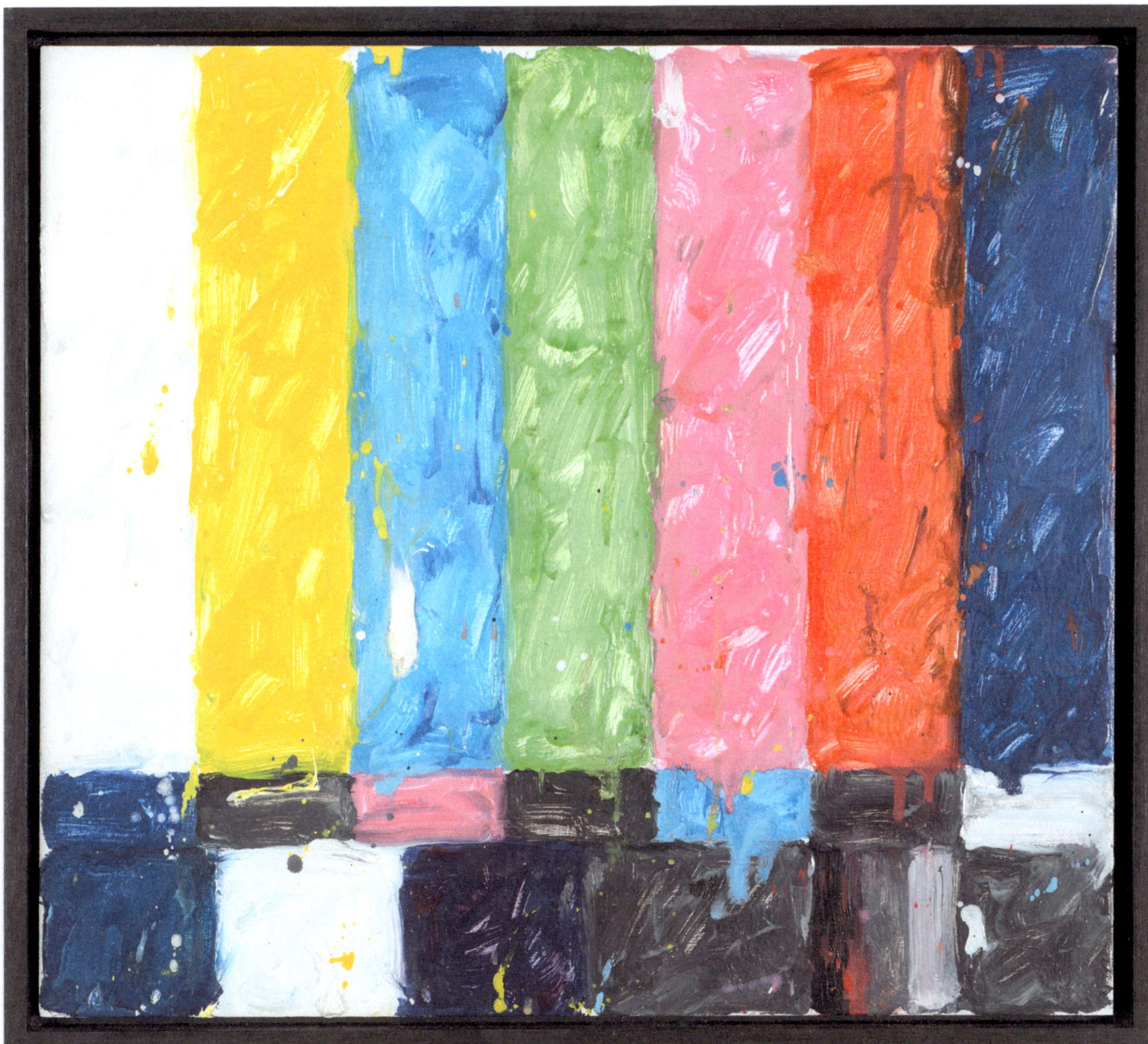

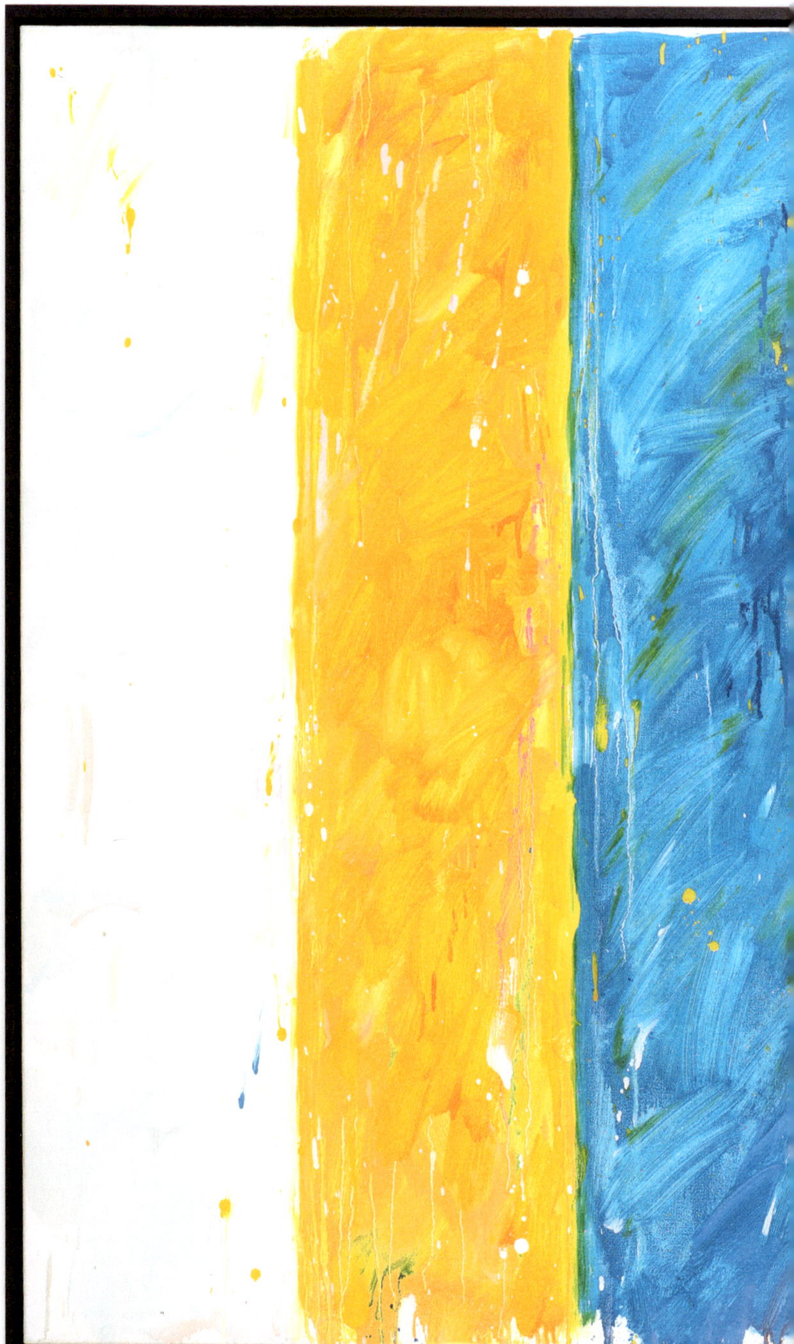

**Testbild / *Test picture***
Öl auf Leinwand / *Oil on canvas*
103,5 x 153,3 cm · 2017

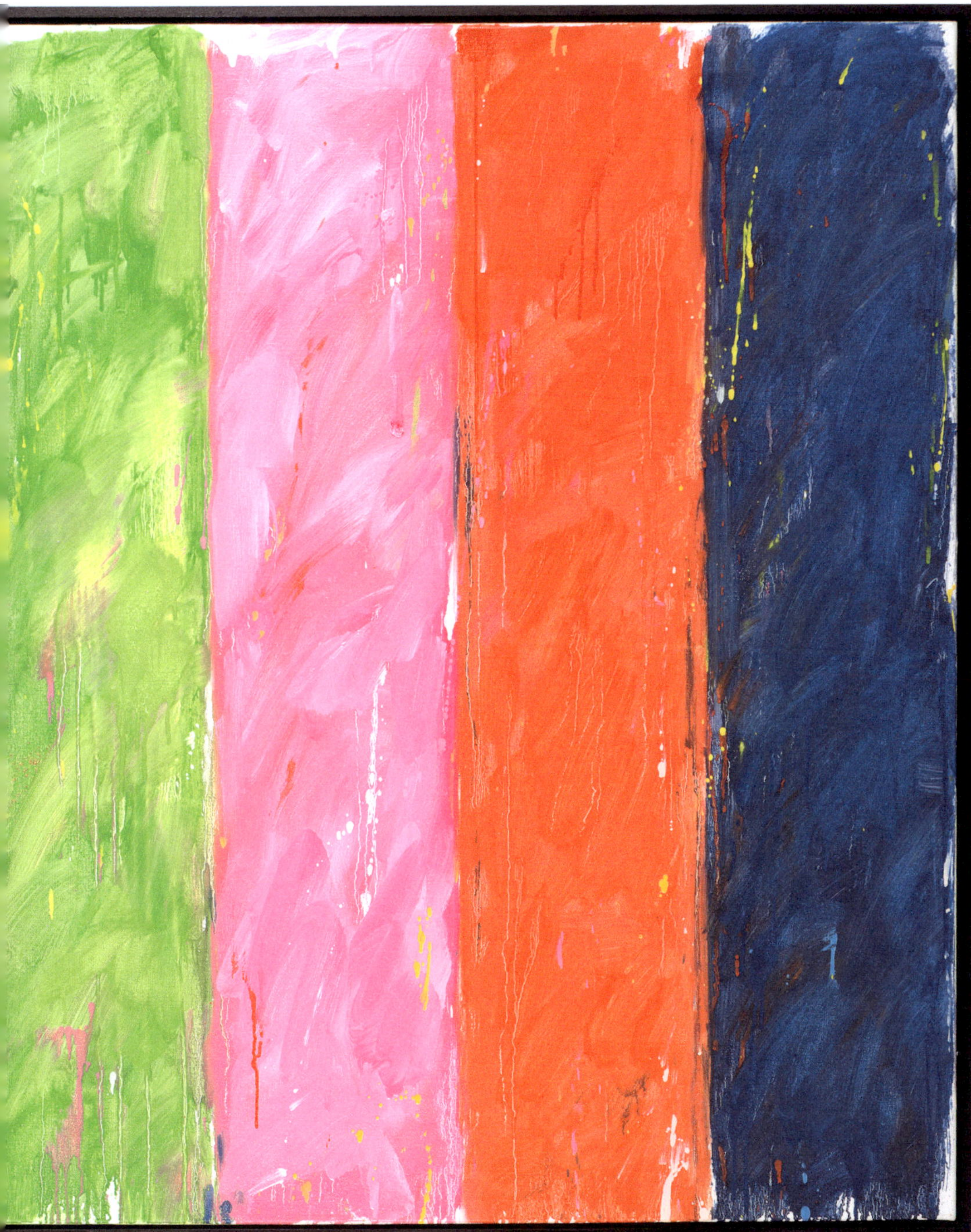

Manchmal muss ich neidvoll anerkennen, dass der Zufall der bessere Gestalter ist.
Dann tröste ich mich damit, dass ich es zumindest bemerkt habe.
*Sometimes I have to jealously admit that chance is the better designer.*
*Then I console myself with the fact that I noticed that, at least.*

**White noise**
Rahmen, Passepartout, Glas
*Frame, passe-partout, glass*
81 x 80 cm · 2017

WHITE NOISE
Armin Lindauer
2017

**Selfcontrol Color**
links: Acryl und Siebdruck auf Nessel auf Hartfaserplatte
rechts: Öl auf Nessel auf Hartfaserplatte
*left: Acryl and silk screen print on nettle cloth on hardboard*
*right: Oil on nettle cloth on hardboard*
180 x 54 cm je Tafel/*per panel* · 1991

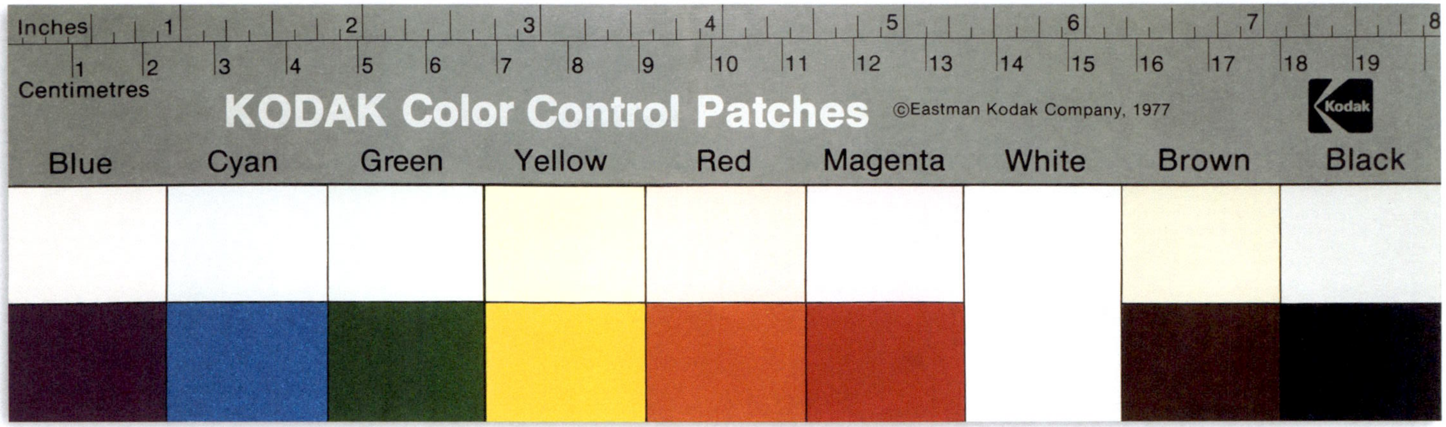
Inches
Centimetres
KODAK Color Control Patches
©Eastman Kodak Company, 1977
Kodak
Blue
Cyan
Green
Yellow
Red
Magenta
White
Brown
Black

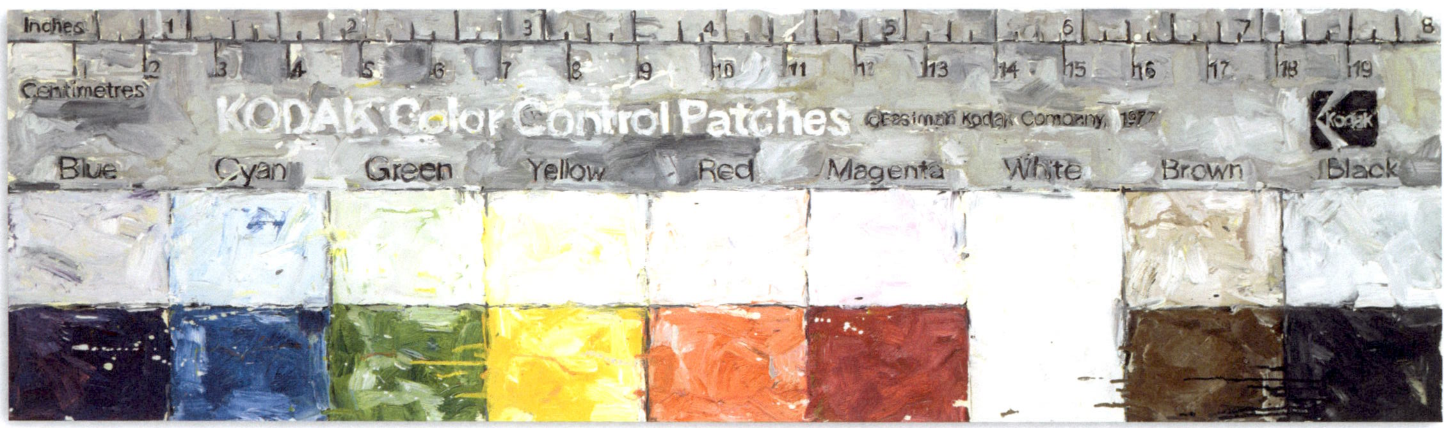
Inches
Centimetres
KODAK Color Control Patches
Blue
Cyan
Green
Yellow
Red
Magenta
White
Brown
Black

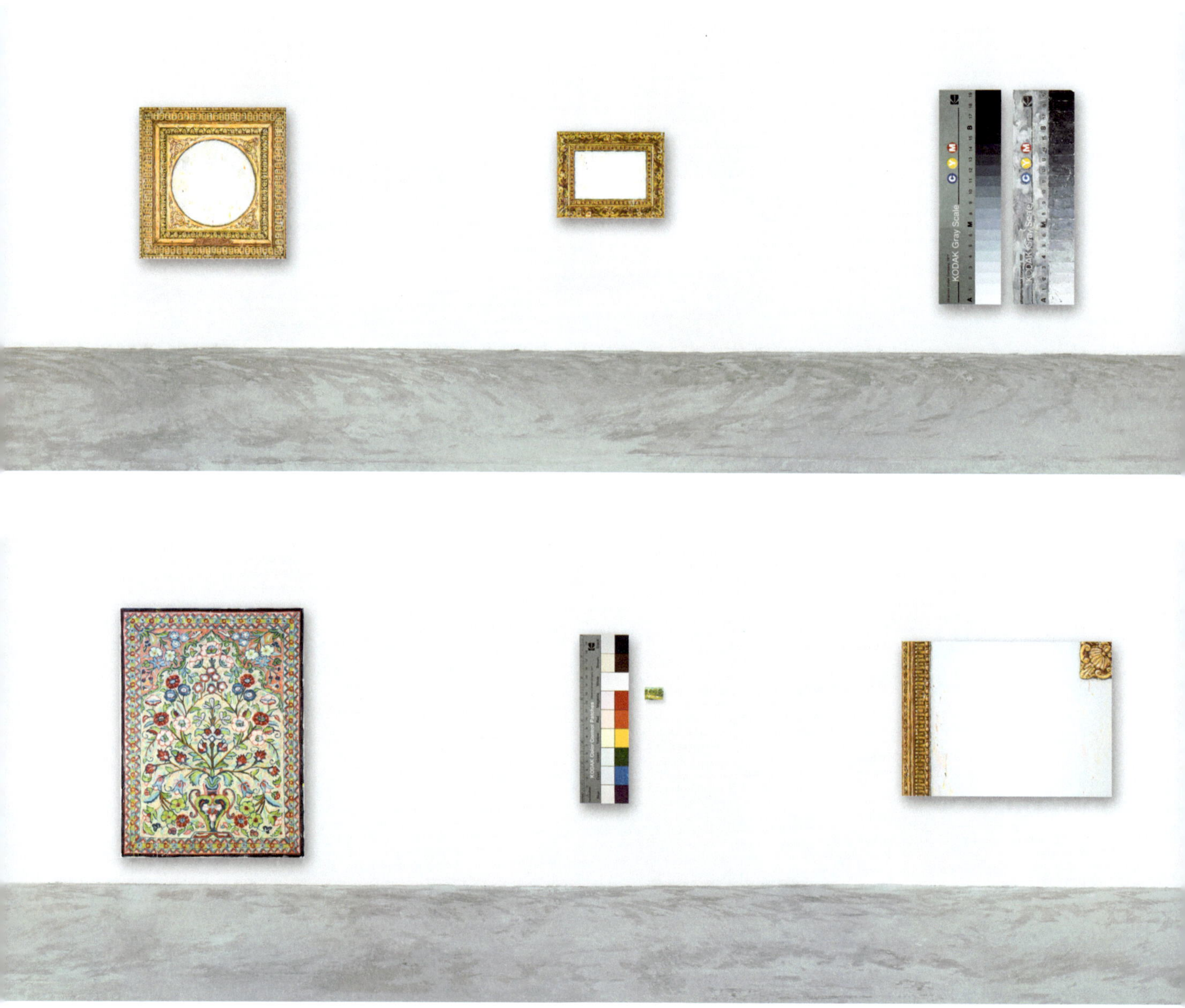
KODAK Gray Scale

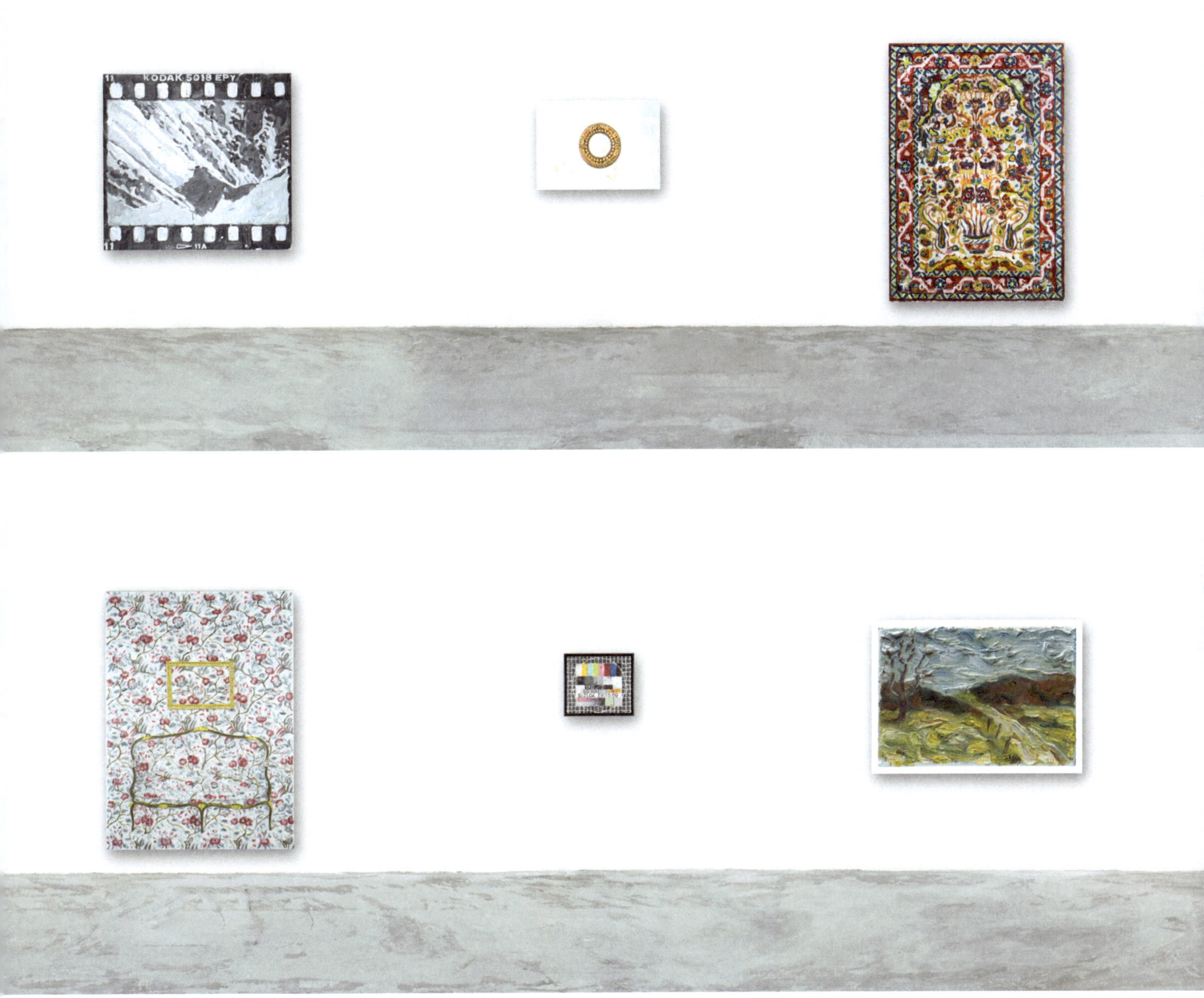


Du sollst dir kein Bild machen«, Artspace POT 72 Berlin, Ausstellungsansicht / *»You shall not make for yourself an image«, Artspace POT 72 Berlin, Exhibition view*

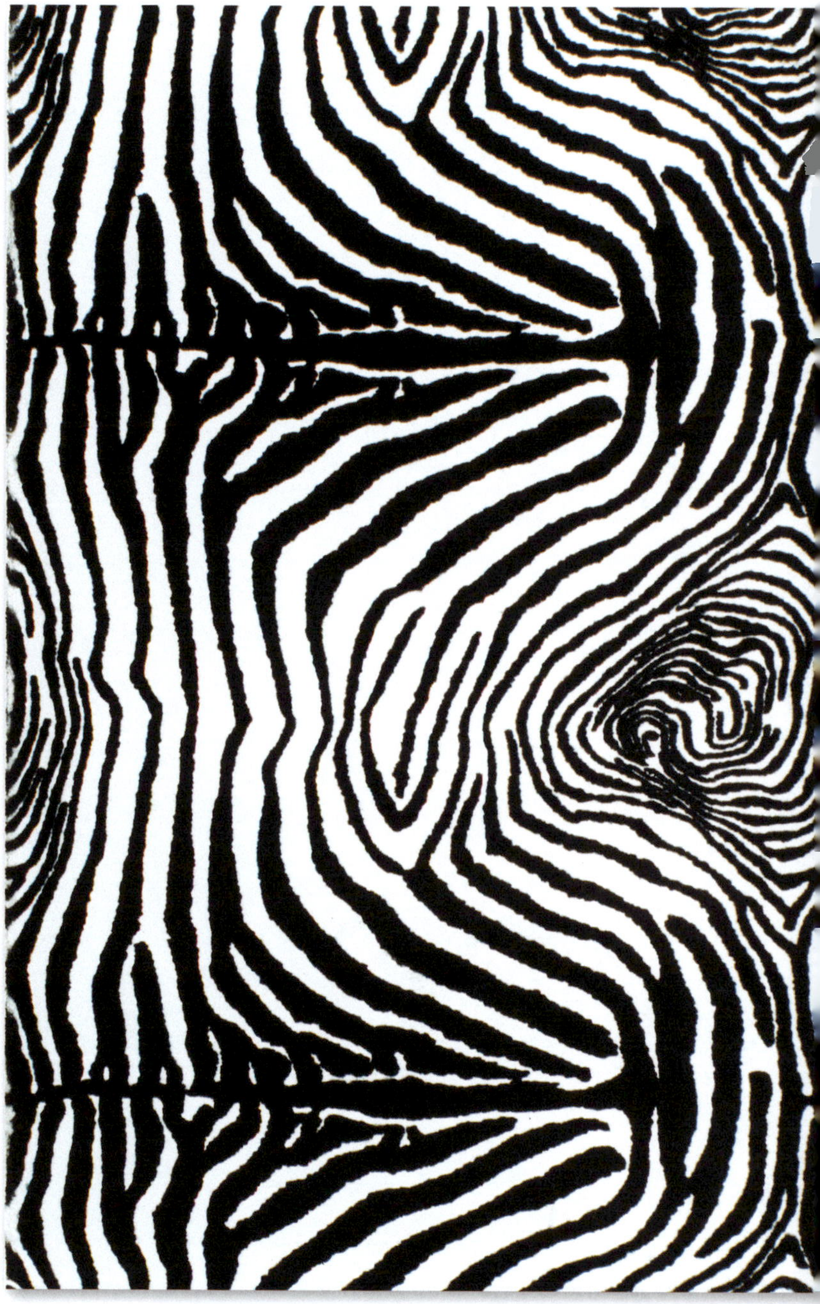

**Kunstfellimitat /** ***Faux fur imitation***
links: Kunstfell · rechts: Öl auf Nessel
*left: faux fur · right: Oil on nettle cloth*
2 Tafeln je / *2 panels each* 119 x 80 cm · 1987

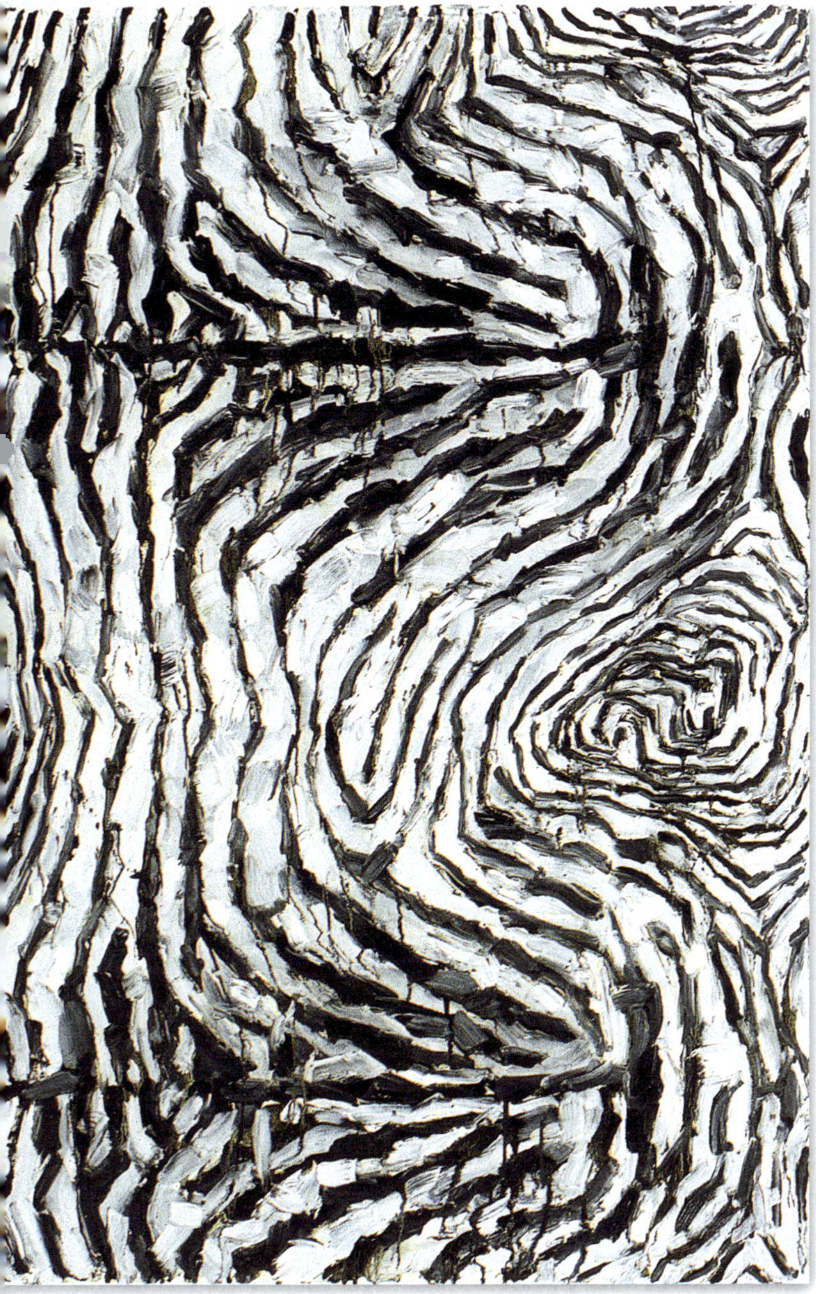

Unlogik und Widersinniges dürfen beim Arbeiten nicht irritieren, im Gegenteil, sie enthalten Wesentliches.
*Illogic and absurdity must not confuse when you are at work; on the contrary, they comprise the essence.*

**Der Sammler / *The collector***
Öl auf Leinwand / *Oil on canvas*
200 x 150 cm · 2012

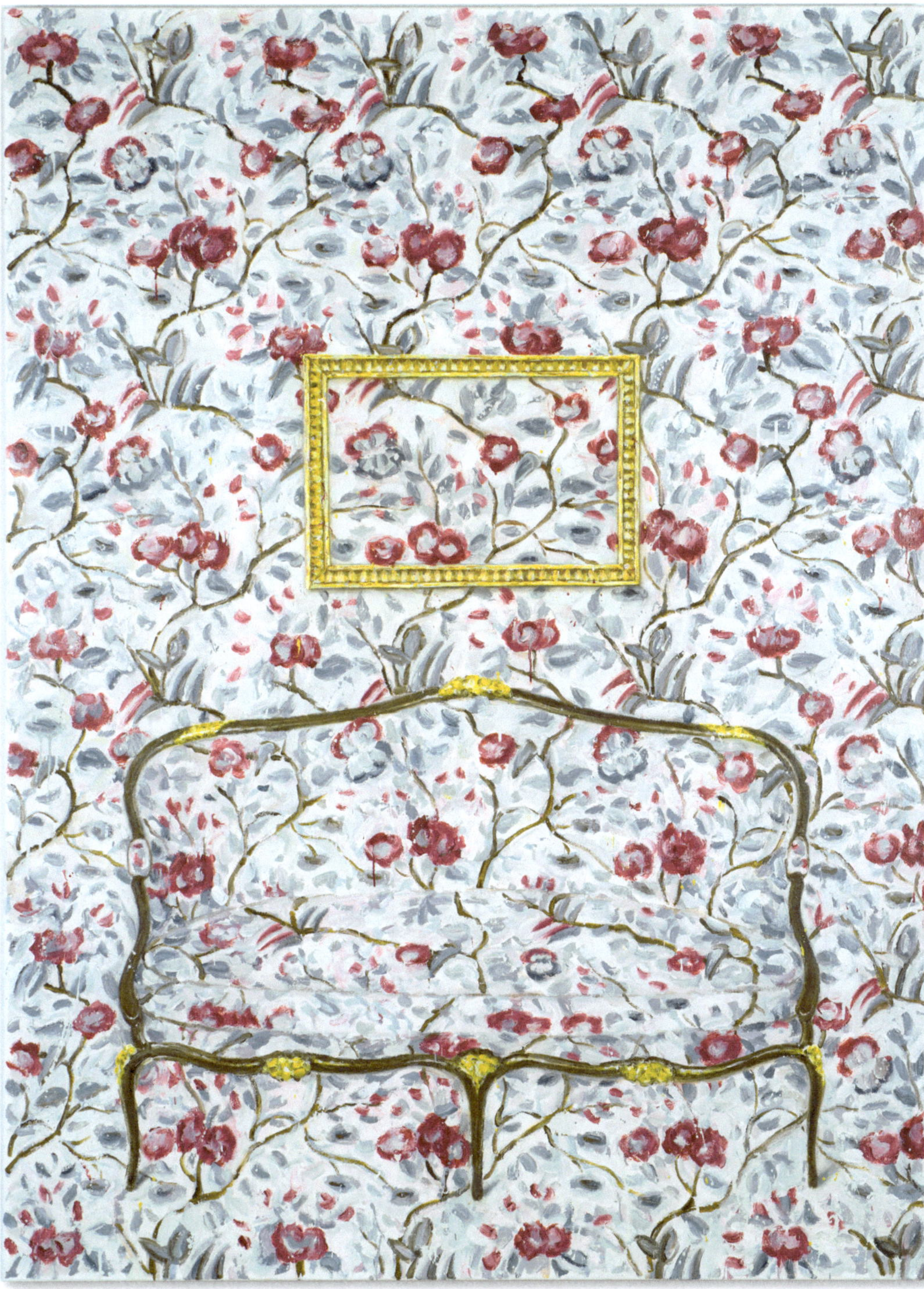

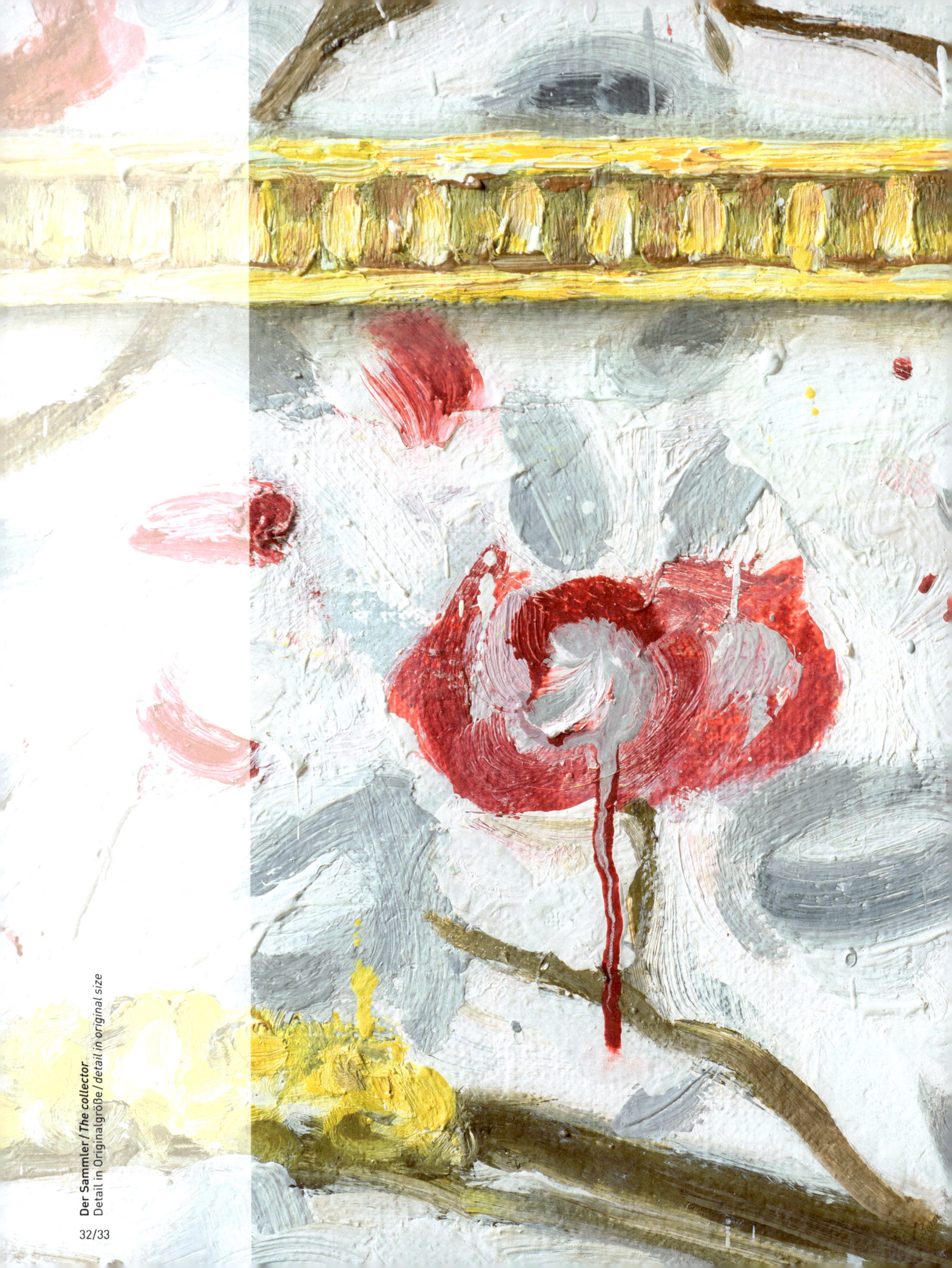

**Der Sammler** / ***The collector***
Detail in Originalgröße / *detail in original size*

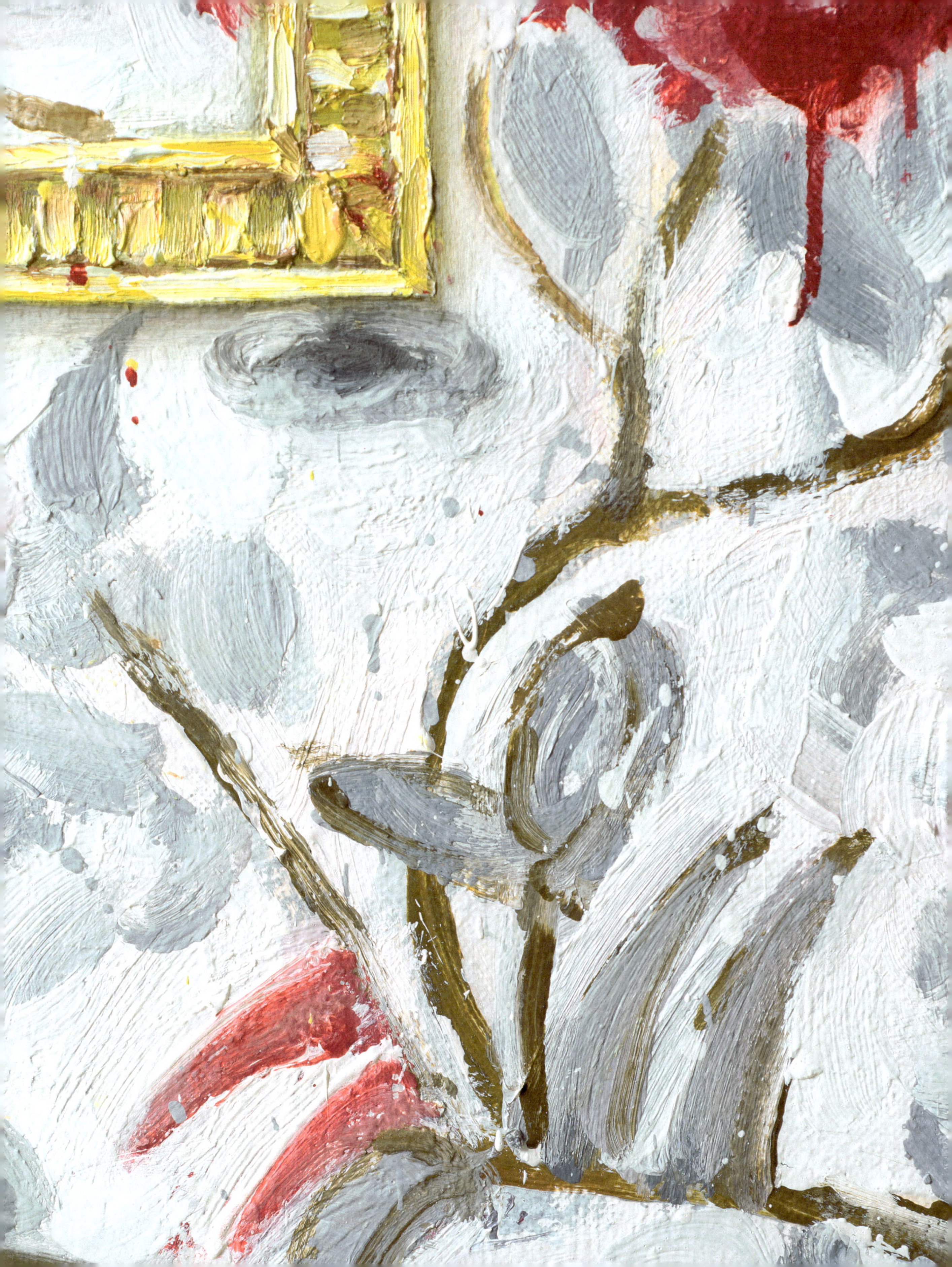

**Der Salonlöwe / *The lounge lizard***
Öl auf Leinwand / *Oil on canvas*
200 x 150 cm · 2013

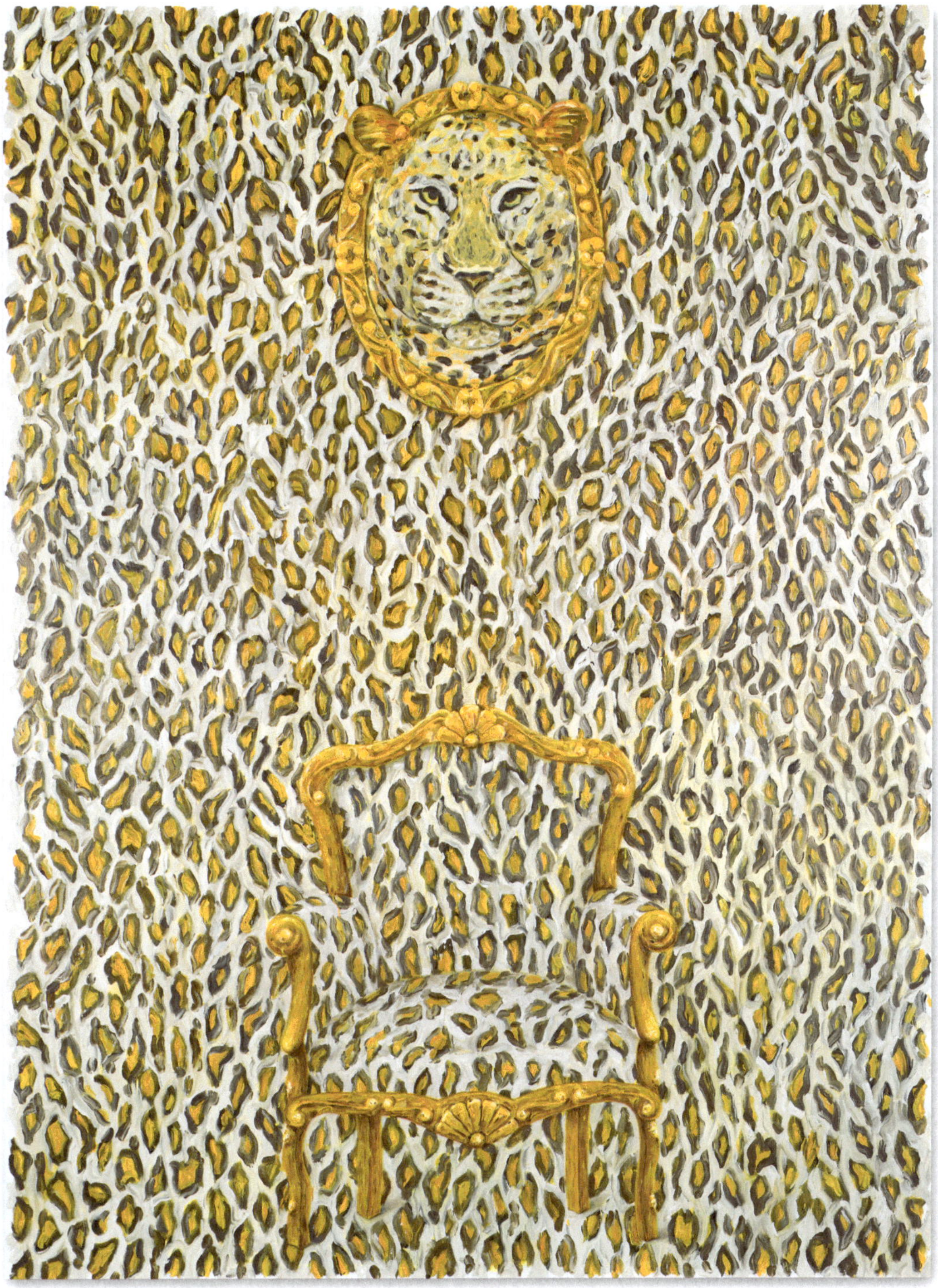

**unvollendet** / ***unfinished***
Keilrahmen, Leinwand, Knochenleim, Keile, Pinsel, Kohle
*Stretcher frame, canvas, bone glue, wedges, brush, charcoal*
140 x 50 cm · 2014

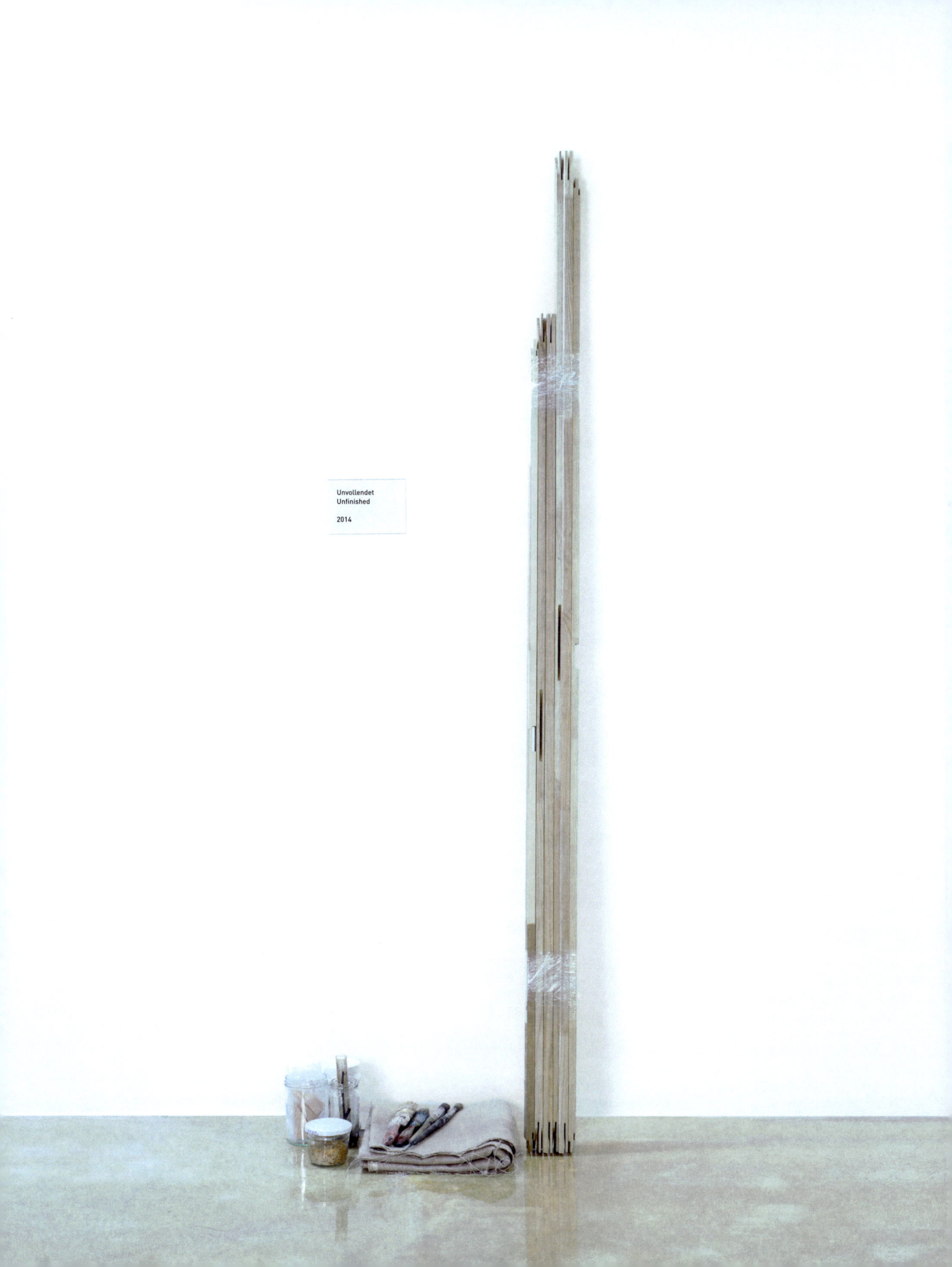
Unvollendet
Unfinished
2014

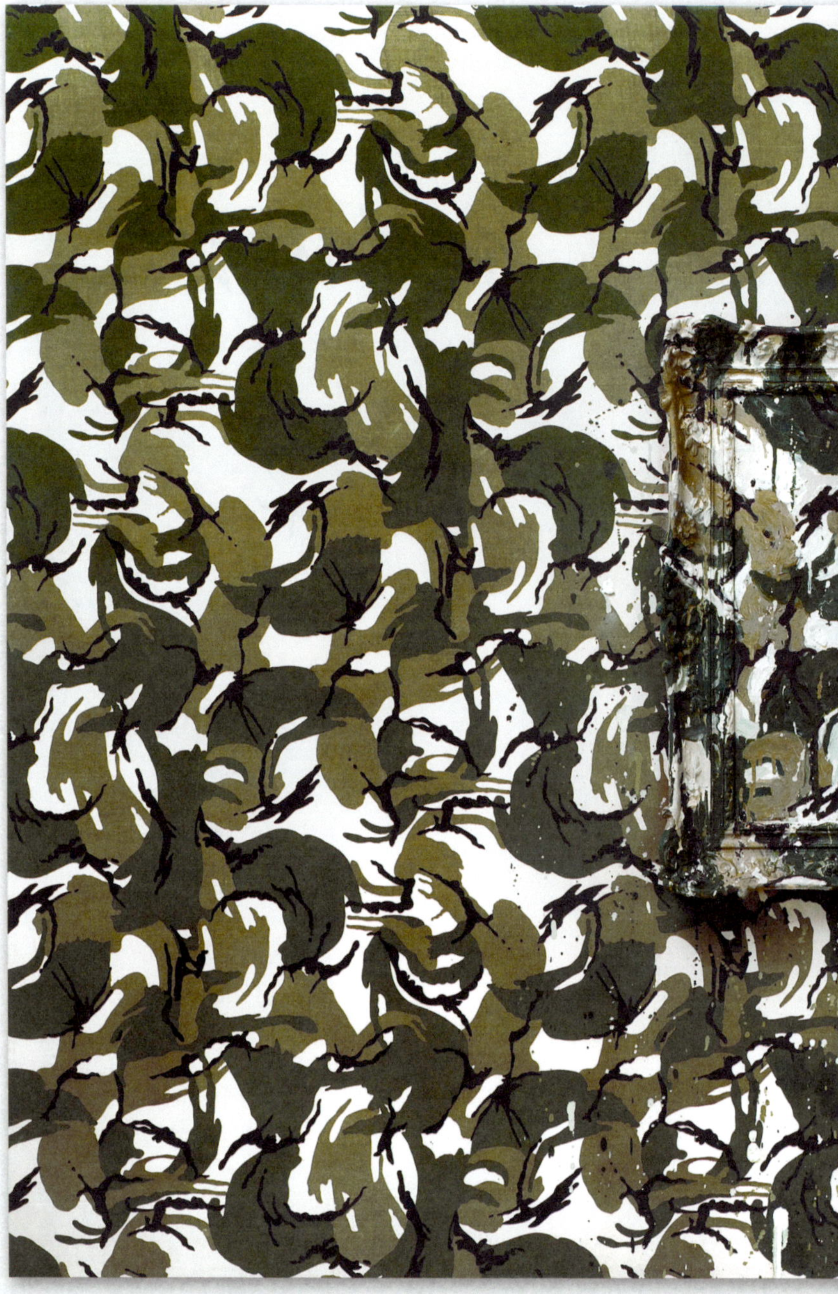

**Tarnbild / *Camouflage picture***
Tarnstoff, Rahmen, Ölfarbe
*Camouflage material, frame, Oil paint*
145 x 210 cm · 2012

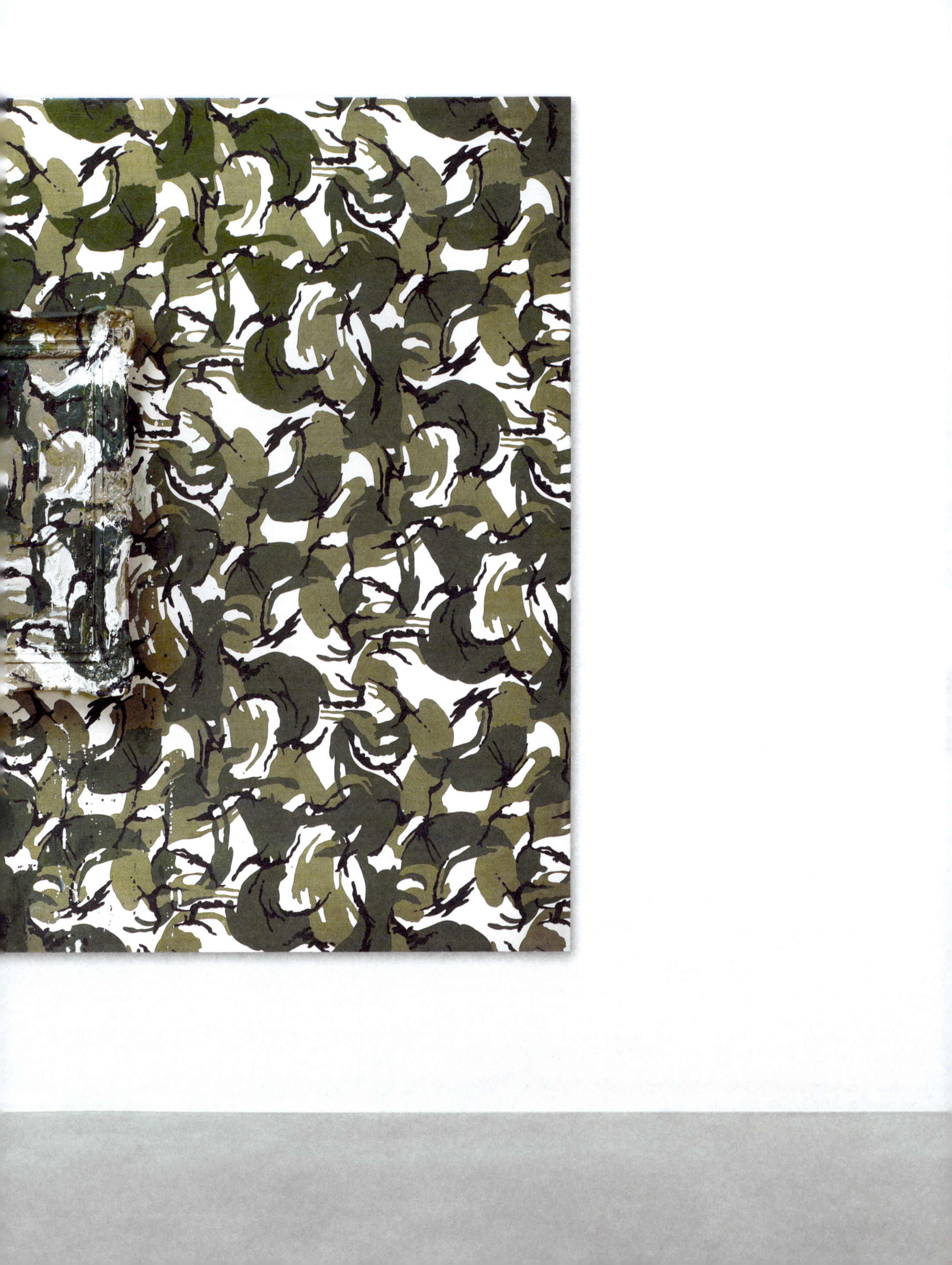

Dass weniger mehr ist, ist prinzipiell richtig.
Nur, dass das Wenige dann verdammt richtig sein muss, sagt niemand.
*That less is more is in principle true.*
*Only, nobody tells you that the less has to be damn right.*

**Blumenvasenbild / *Flower vase picture***
Öl auf Leinwand / *Oil on canvas*
100 x 148 cm · 2013

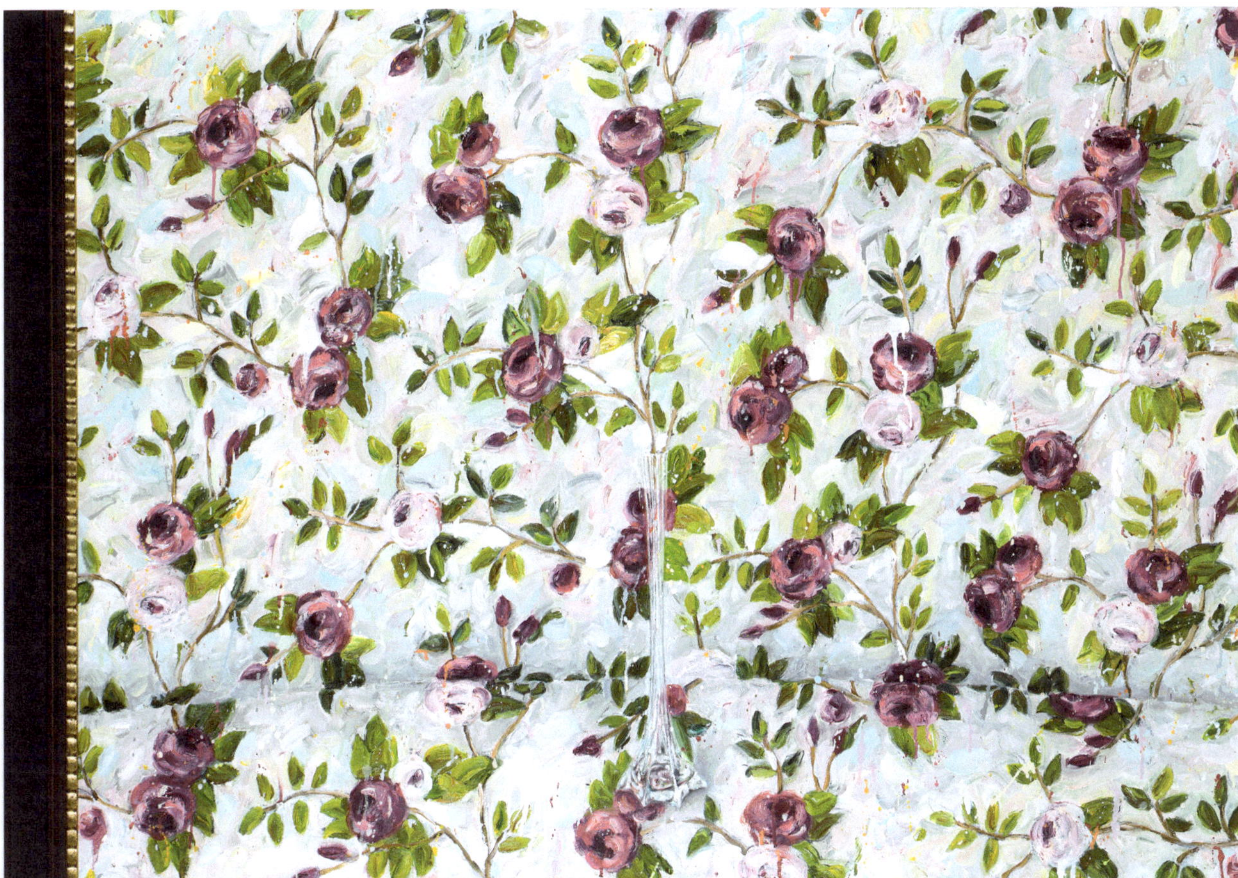

Bei manchen Bildern sieht Absicht wie Zufall,
bei anderen Zufall wie Absicht aus.
Das ist ein interessantes Phänomen.
*In some images intention looks like chance*
*in others chance looks like intention.*
*That's an interesting phenomenon.*

**vorBilder / *Role models***
Öl auf Hartfaserplatte auf Tapete auf Tischlerplatte
*Oil on hardboard on wallpaper on core-board*
100 x 70 cm · 2005

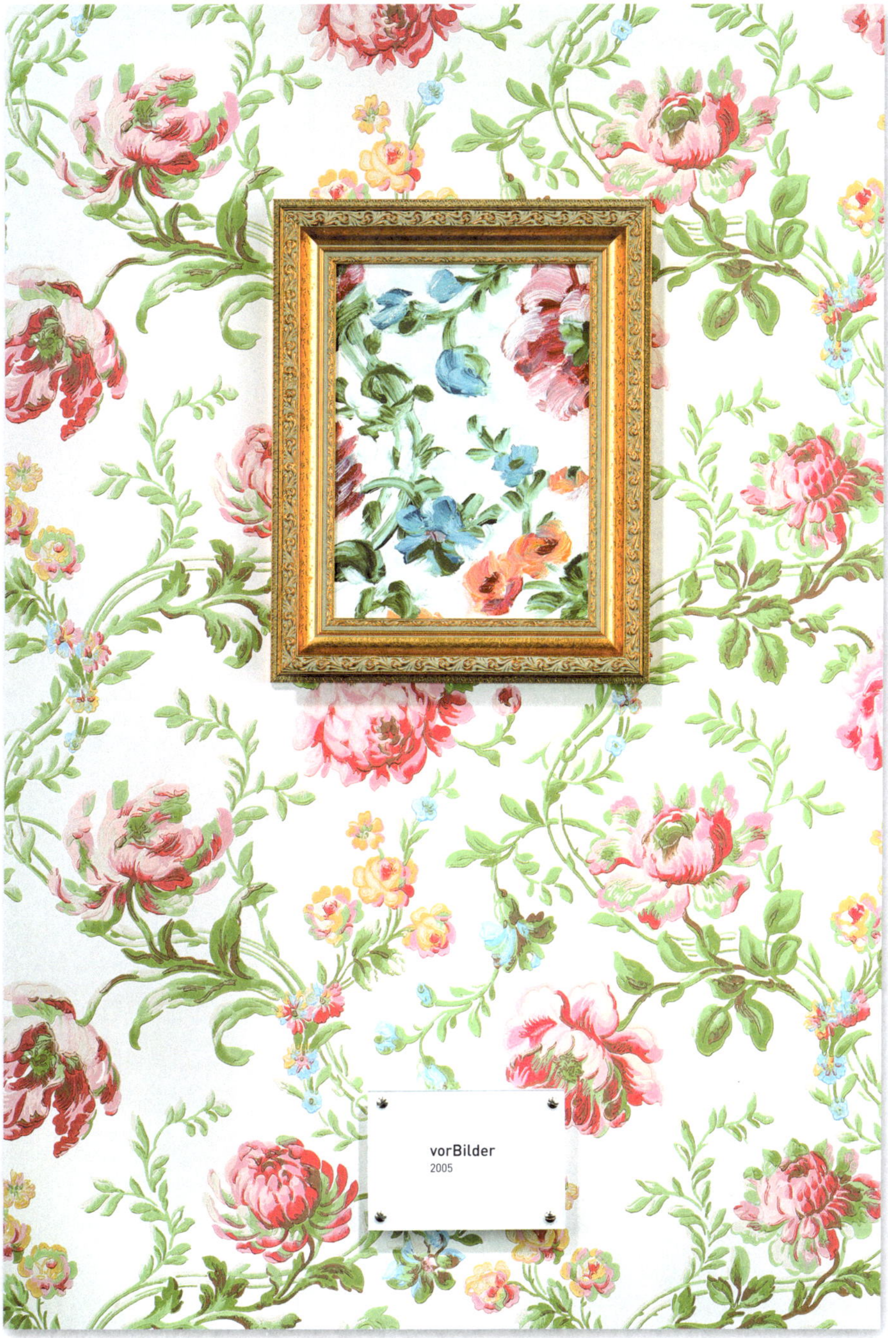
vorBilder
2005

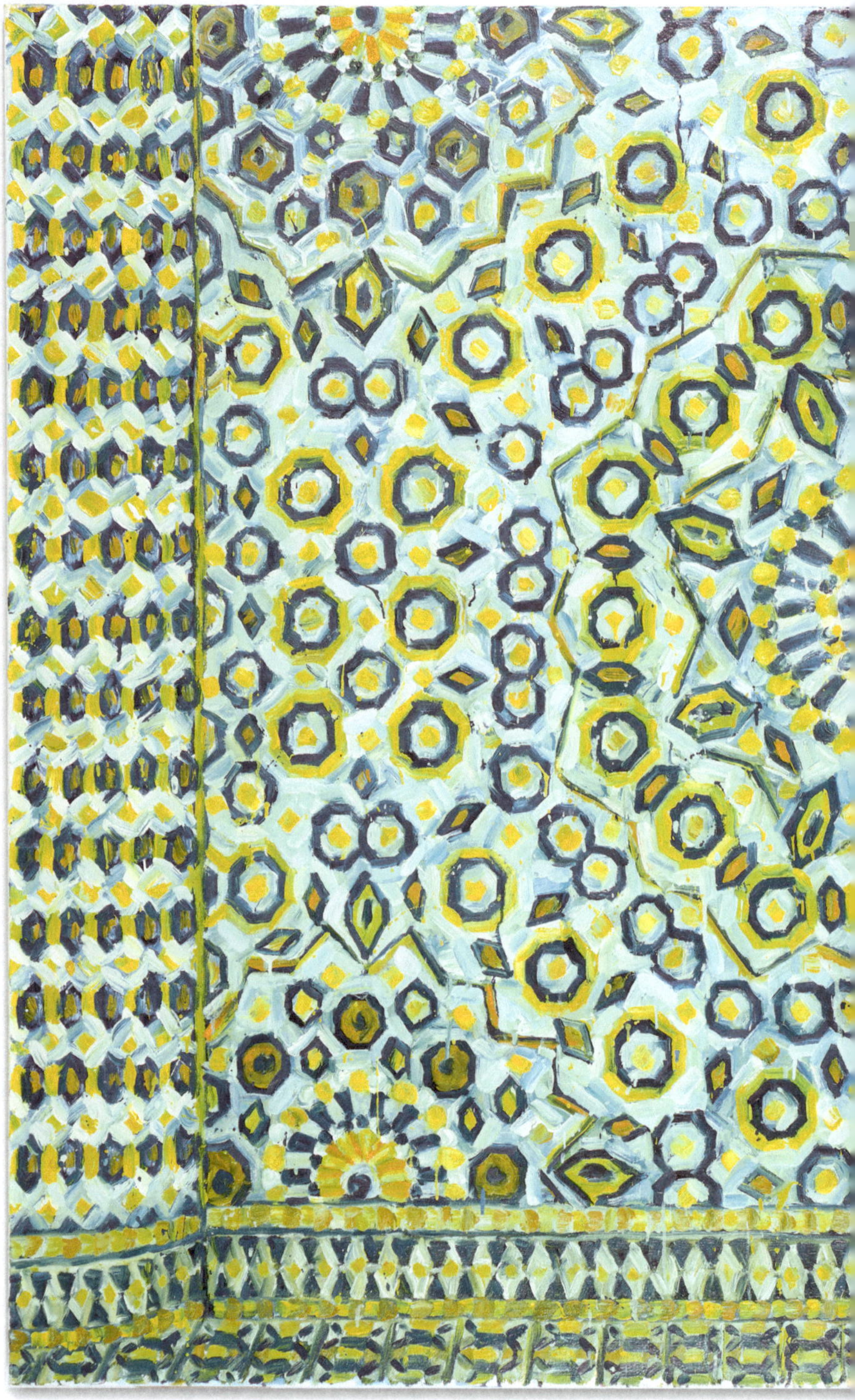

**Orientierung**/*Orientation*
Öl auf Leinwand/*Oil on canvas*
150 x 200 cm · 2012

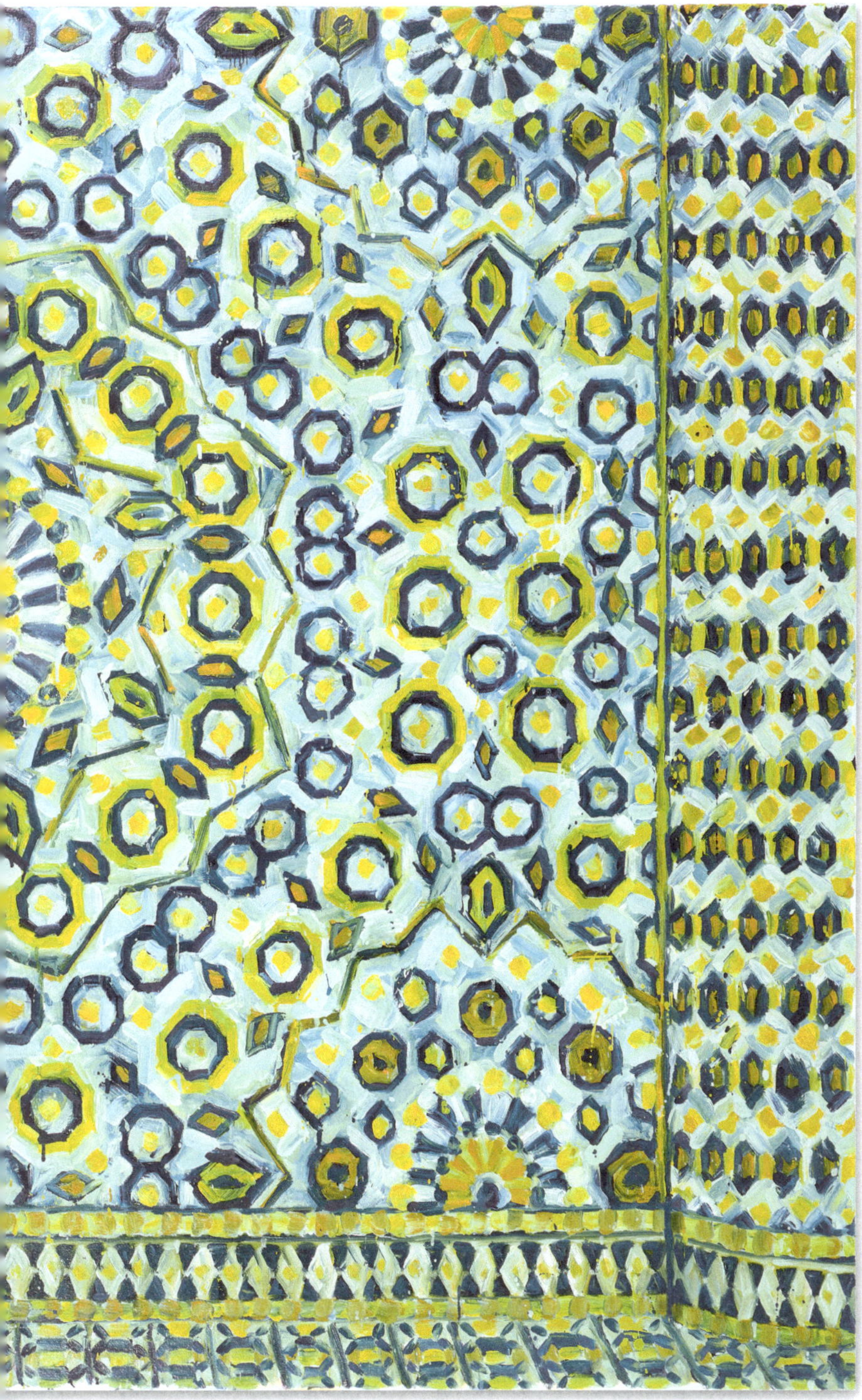

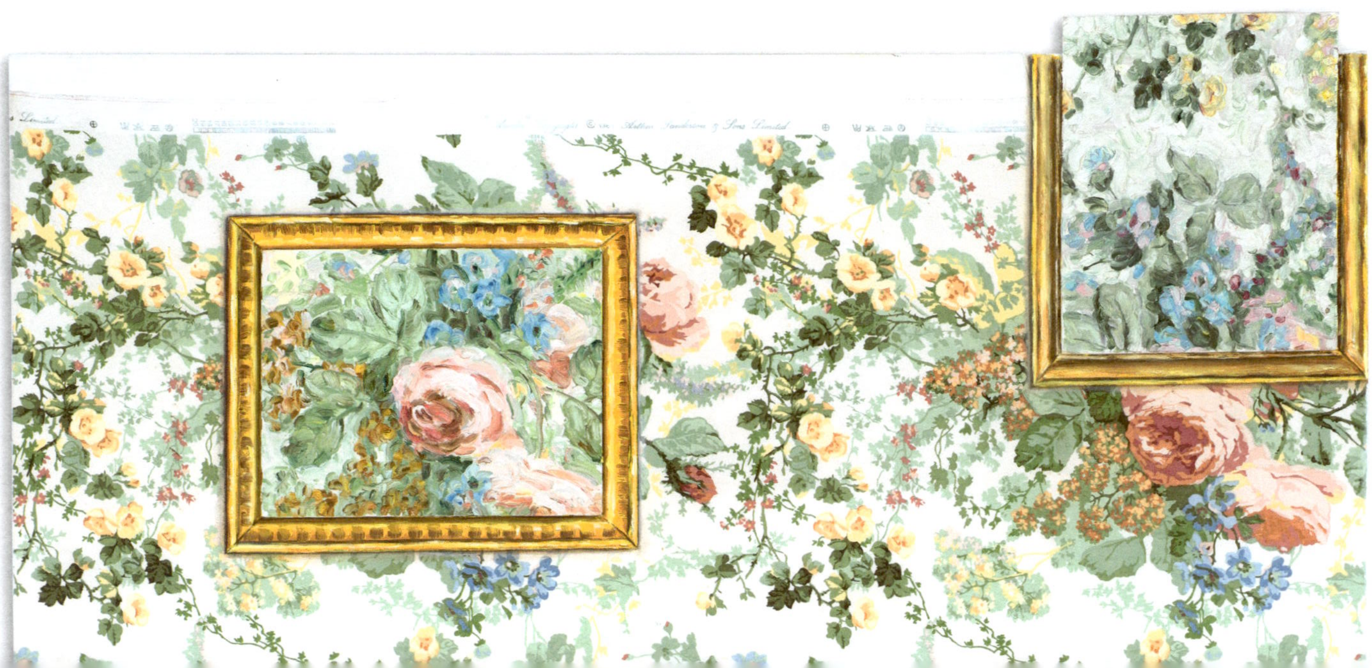

**Blumentapetenbild** / ***Floral wallpaper picture***
Öl auf Hartfaserplatten auf Stofftapete auf Nessel
*Oil on hardboard on fabric wallpaper on nettle cloth*
120 x 159 cm · 2013/2017

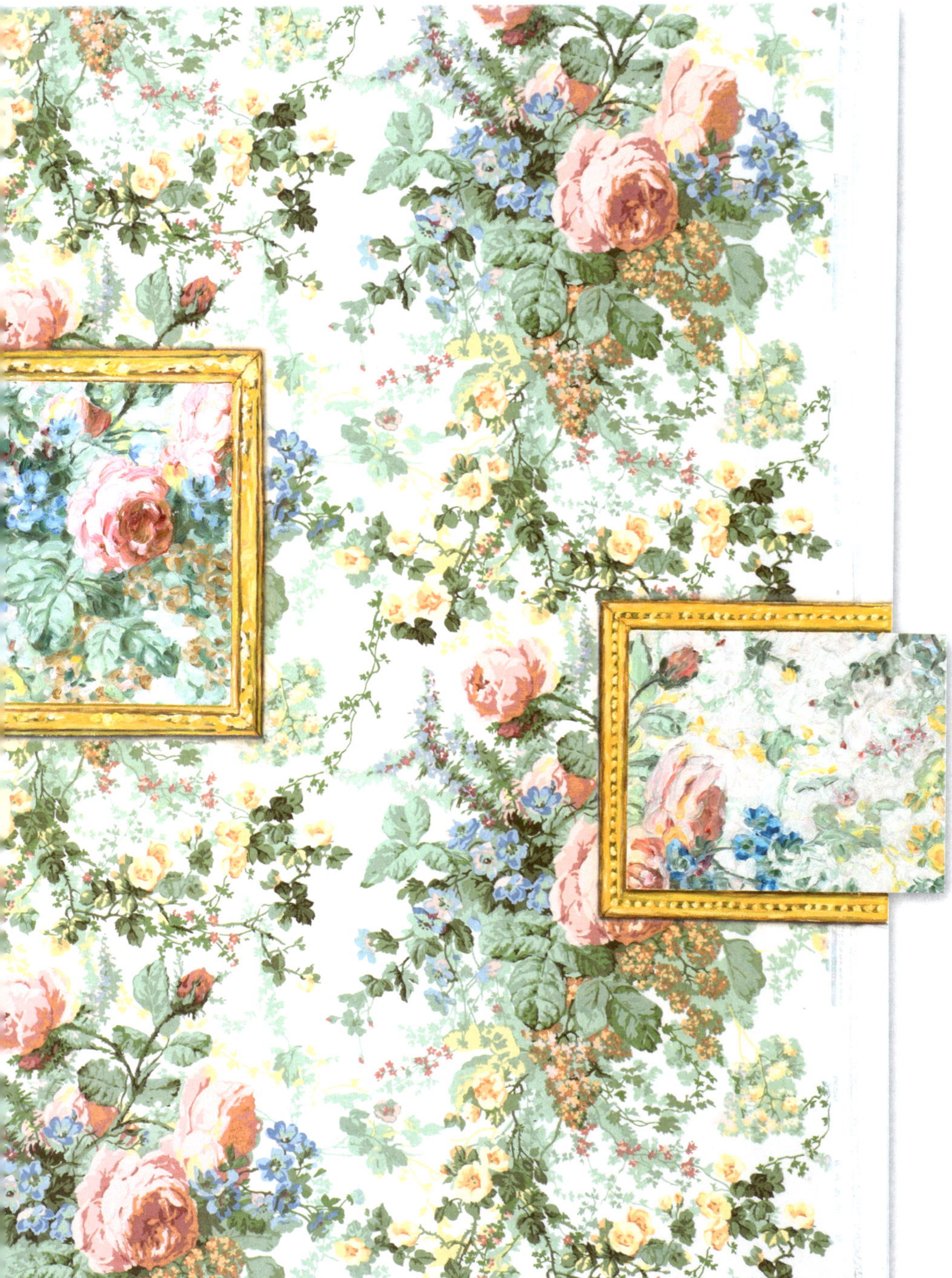

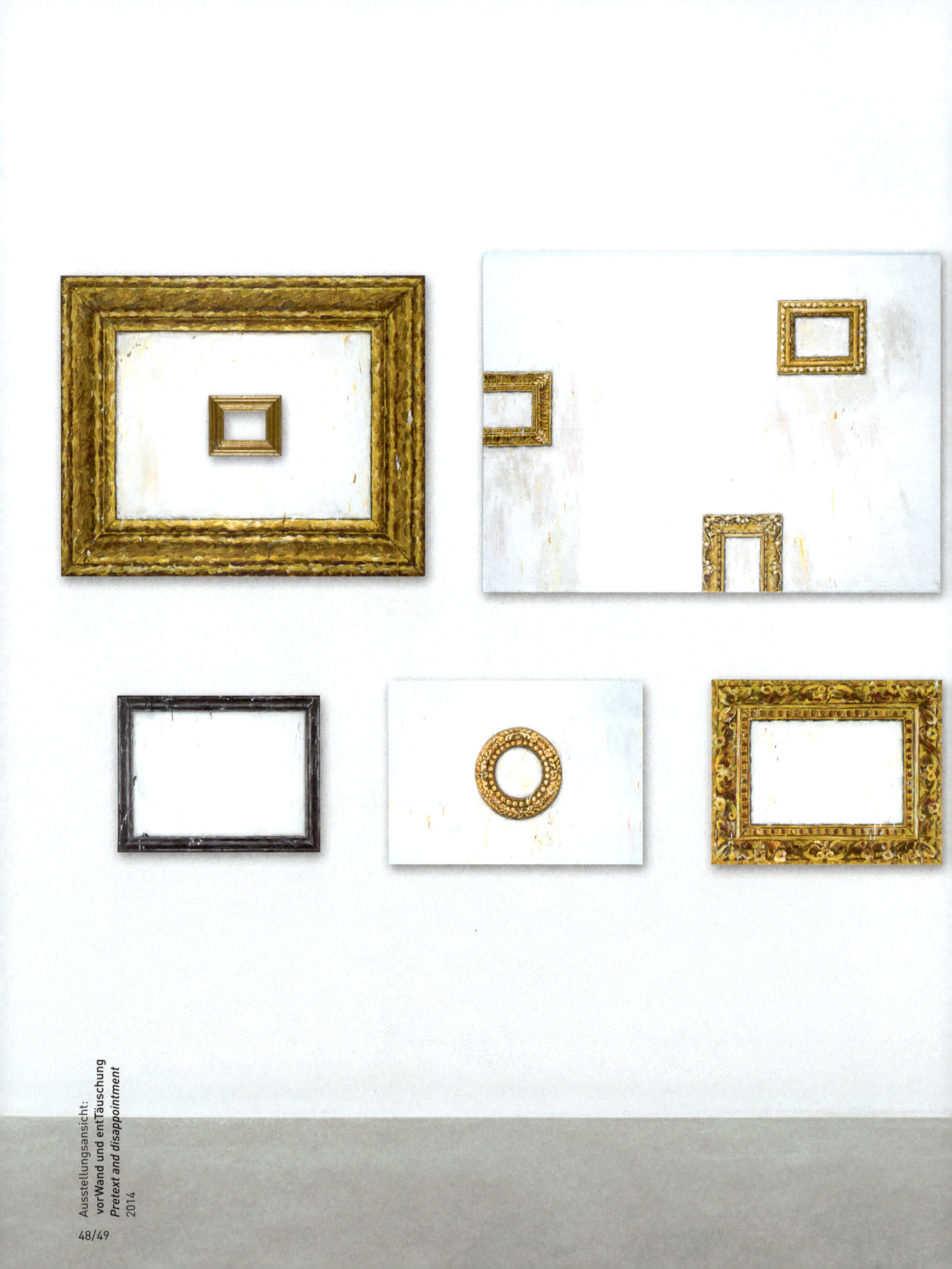

Ausstellungsansicht:
**vorWand und entTäuschung**
*Pretext and disappointment*
2014

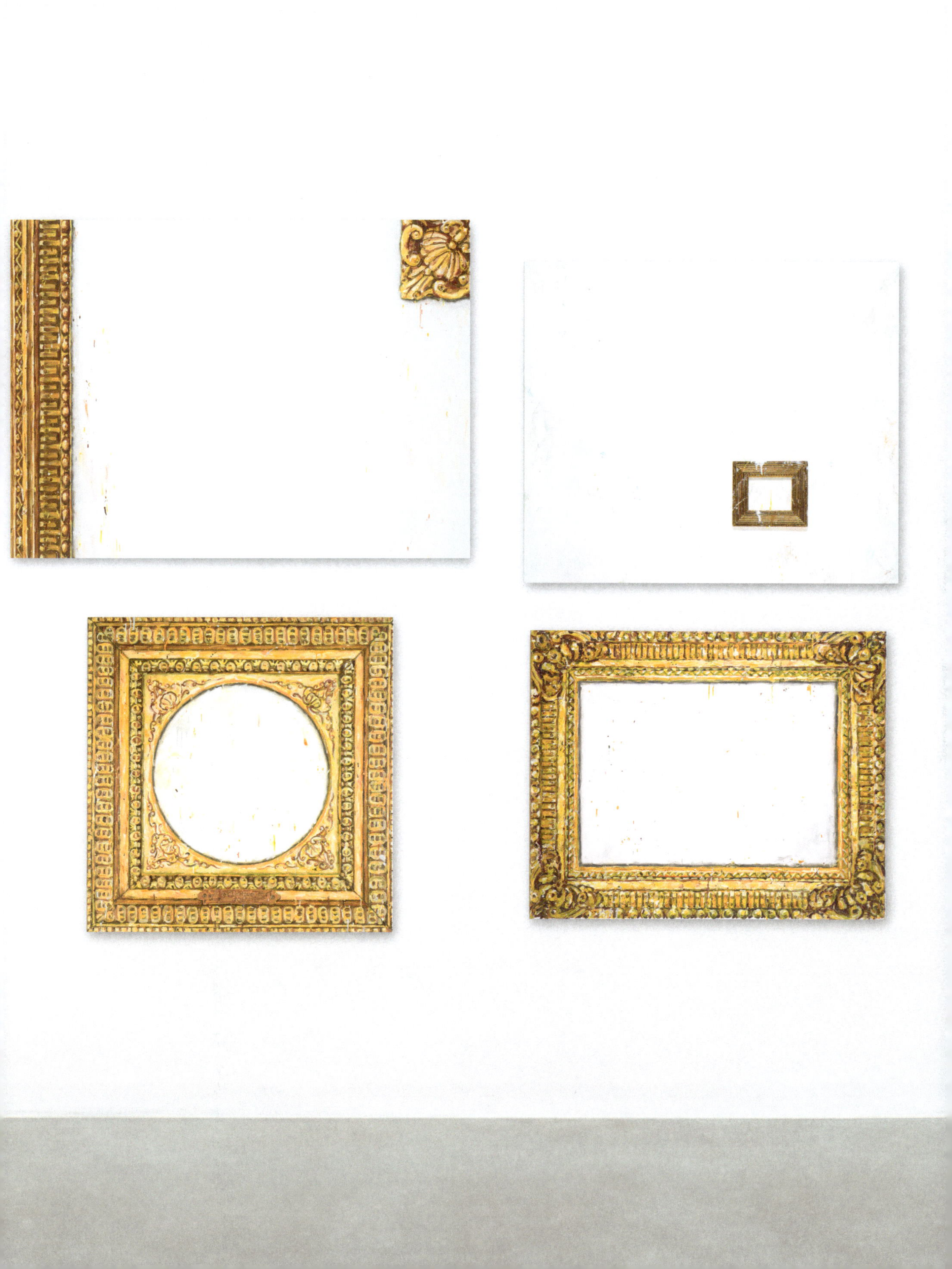

**Rahmenbild / *Frame picture***
Öl auf Leinwand / *Oil on canvas*
70 x 90 cm · 2013

**Einfache Gestaltung ist teuflisch kompliziert zu machen.**
*Simple design is devilishly complicated to do.*

**Rahmenbild** / ***Frame picture***
Öl auf Leinwand / *Oil on canvas*
70 x 100 cm · 2013

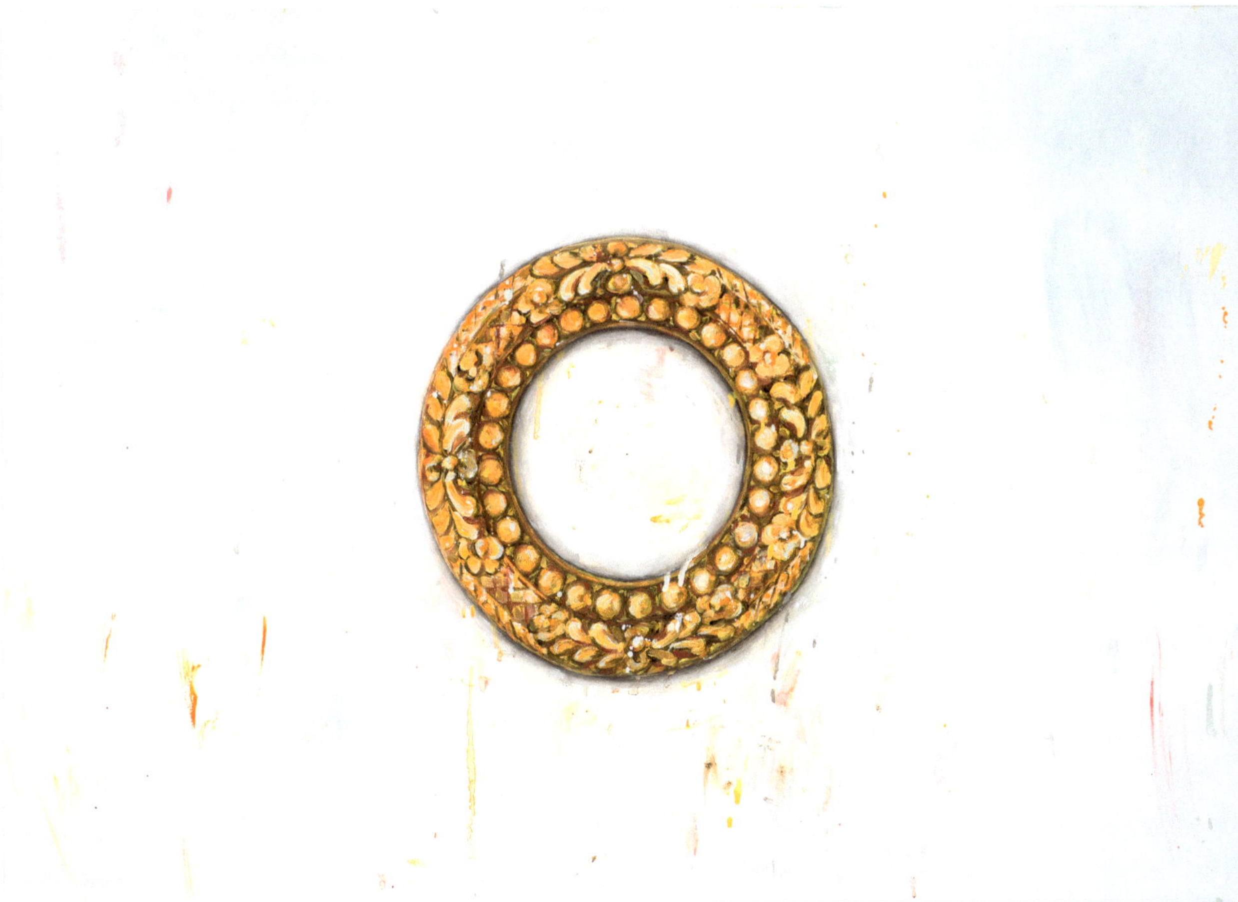

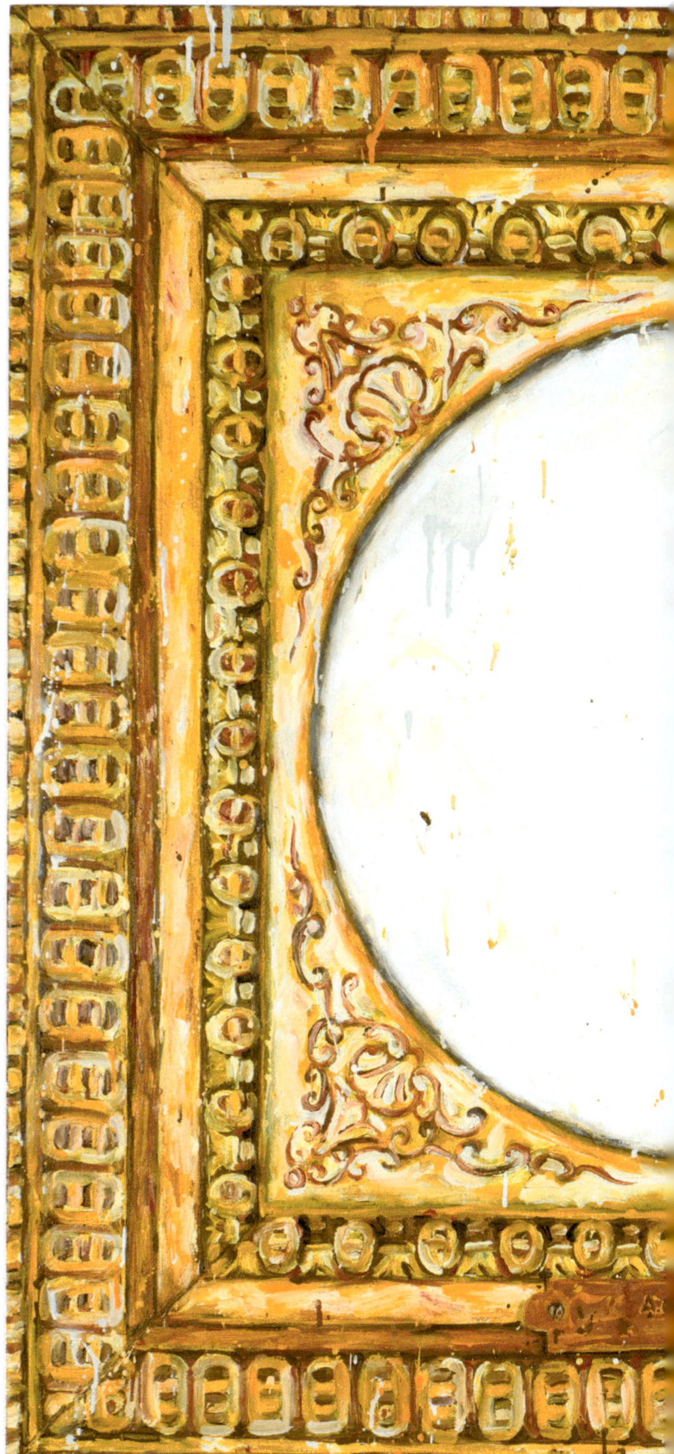

**Rahmenbild / *Frame picture***
Öl auf Leinwand / *Oil on canvas*
120 x 120 cm · 2012

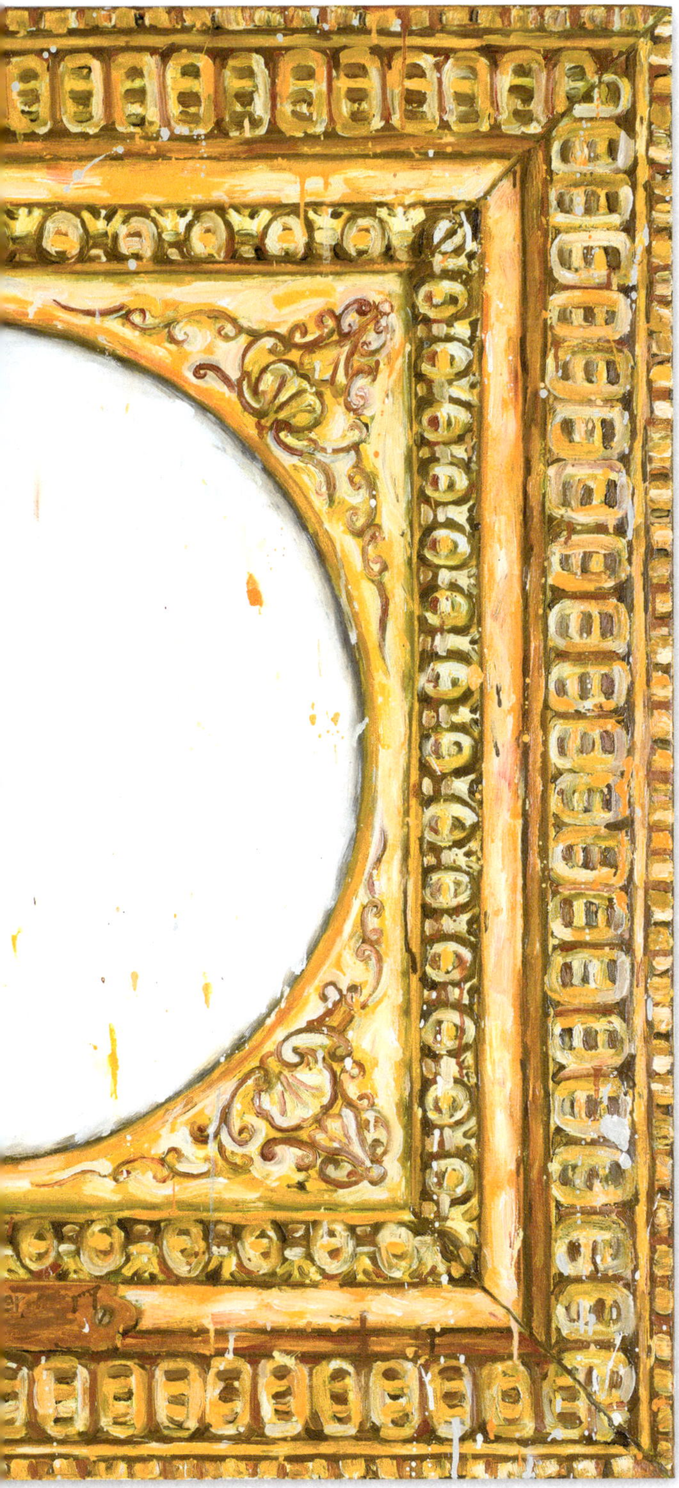

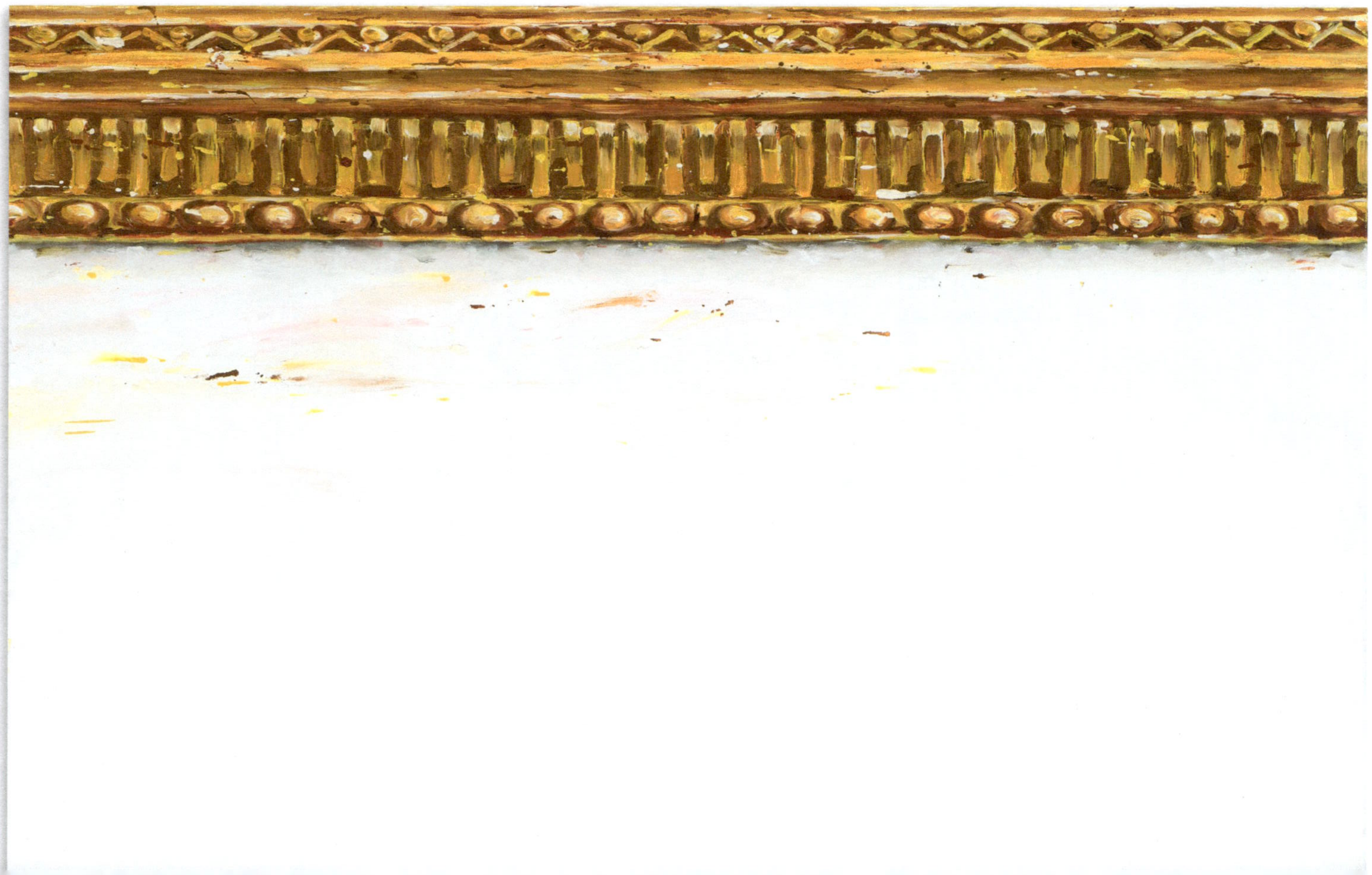

**Rahmenbild /** ***Frame picture***
Öl auf Leinwand / *Oil on canvas*
130 x 180 cm · 2013

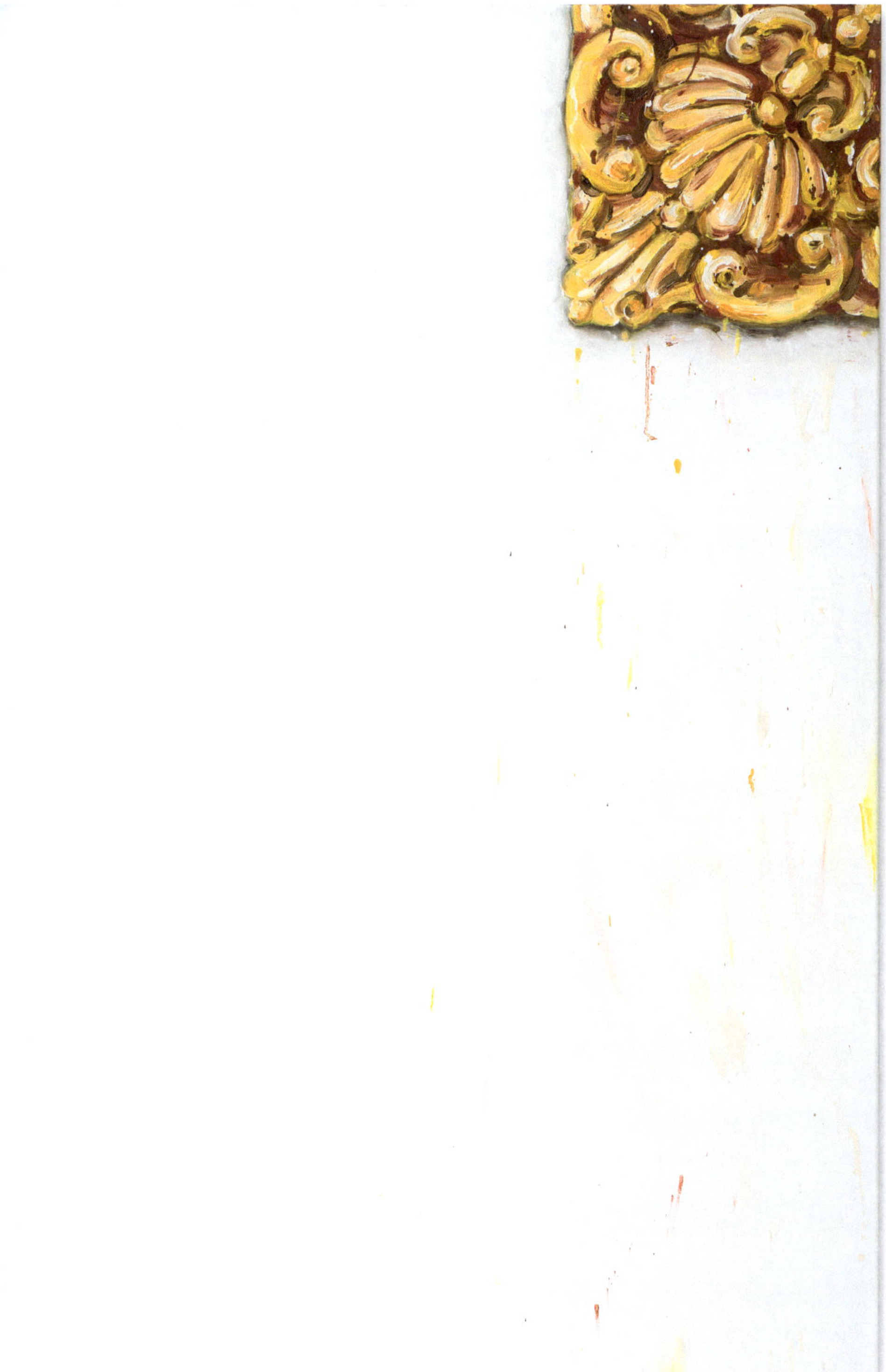

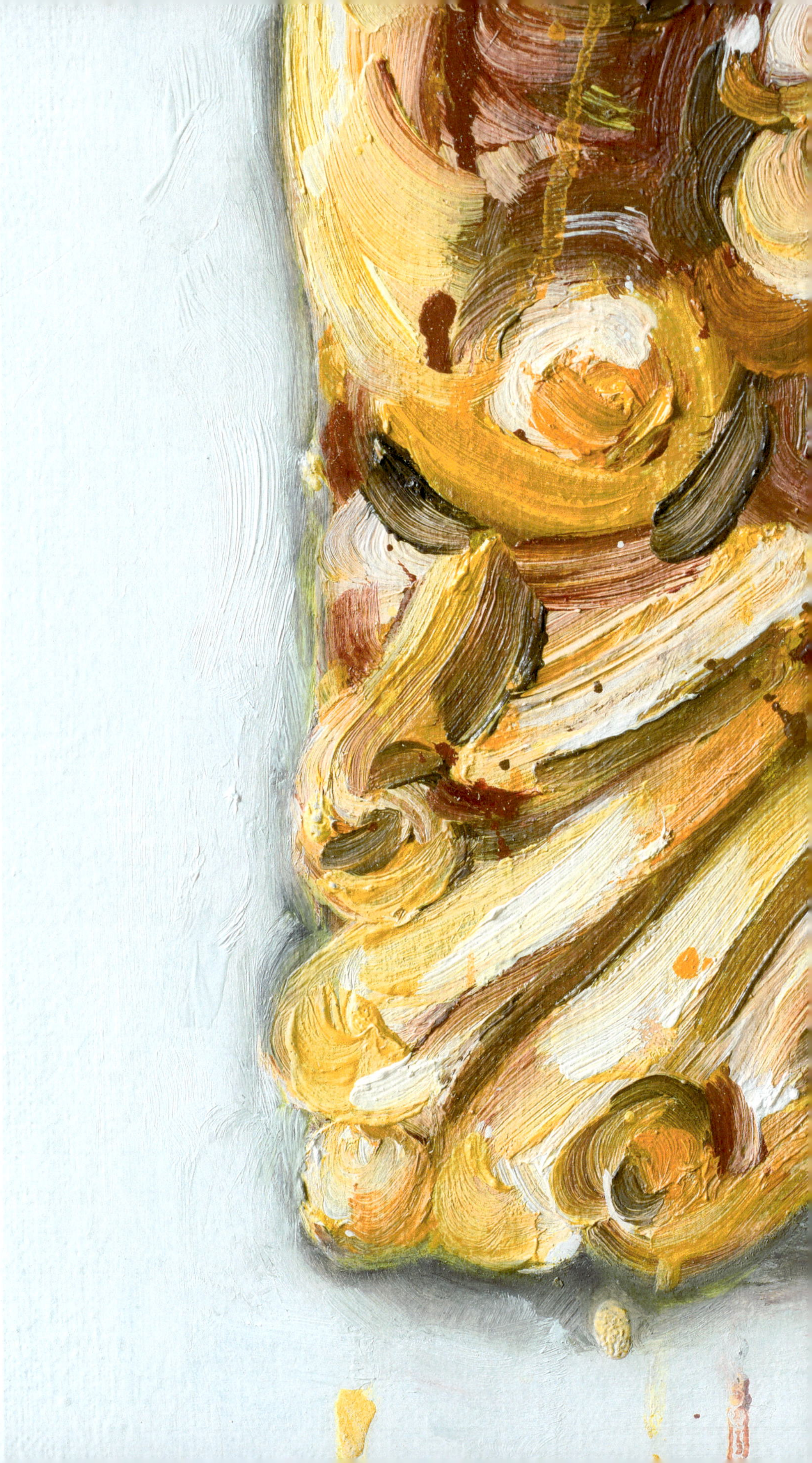

**Rahmenbild /** ***Frame picture***
Detail in Originalgröße / *detail in original size*

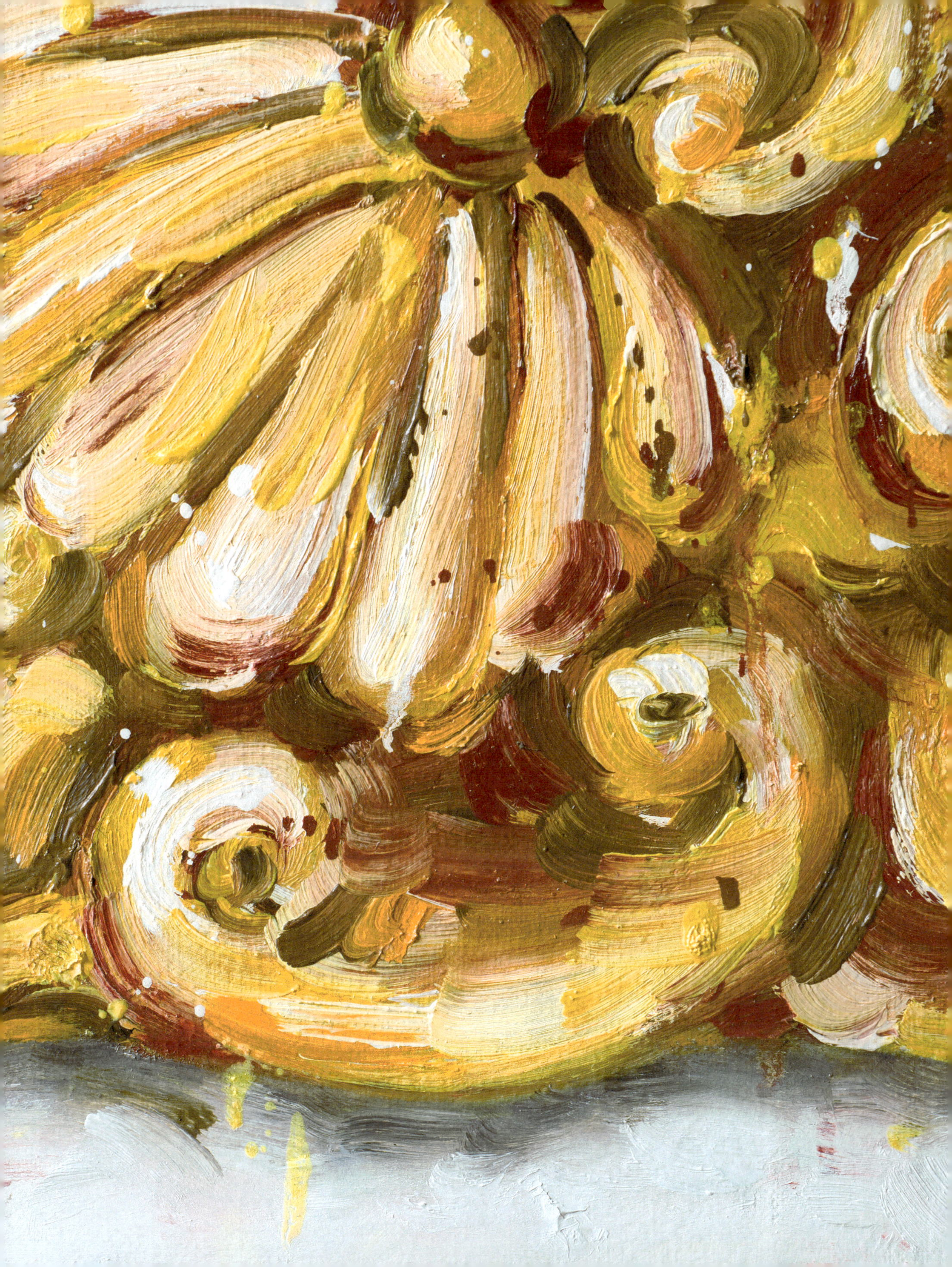

# Malerische Reflexion.

**Thomas Friedrich** // lehrt Designtheorie und Philosophie
an der Hochschule Mannheim

Die künstlerische Moderne beginnt mit einer neuen Fragestellung, die Cézanne begründet hat. Vor seiner Zeit beschäftigten sich die bildenden Künstler jahrhundertlang damit, wie man die Welt und ihre Teile richtig abbilden könne. Freilich wurde stets darüber gestritten, was denn die Welt und ihre Teile nun genau seien und was denn unter »richtig« zu verstehen sei, aber eines war unzweifelhaft, das Bild war Abbild. Als seine Idealform denke man sich ein Renaissancetafelbild, zum Beispiel Las Meninas von Velázquez. Und dann kommt Cézanne, malt den Berg Sainte-Victoire annähernd hundertmal und macht seinem Bruder in einem langen Briefwechsel klar, dass es ihm nicht mehr darum ginge, wie man Natur oder Kultur richtig abbilden würde, sondern ihn treibe die Frage, was denn überhaupt ein Bild sei.

Und genau mit dieser zukunftweisenden Fragestellung wird eine neue Epoche eingeleitet, die bildende Kunst wird reflexiv, wird gleichsam philosophisch, ohne das philosophische Medium theoretischer Texte zu benutzen, sondern die bildnerischen Mittel selbst. Das Vorhergegangene, das Abbild, das Renaissancetafelbild fliegt auseinander, explodiert durch Analyse, wird zerlegt in seine es bestimmenden Einzelteile, wird vernichtet und aufgehoben zugleich, um es hegelianisch auszusprechen. Das ist der Schock der Moderne. Materialistischer Motor für diese Neuaufstellung der bildenden Kunst war die Erfindung der Fotografie im 19. Jahrhundert, ein Medium, das wie nie zuvor die Welt abbilden konnte, was Eugène Delacroix zu der spontanen Aussage verleitete, »die Malerei ist tot«.

Nun war die Basis der abstrakten Kunst gelegt, und ein paar Beispiele der analytischen Resultate sollen hier genannt sein: Kasimir Malewitsch, Paul Klee und Piet Mondrian beschäftigten sich auf je verschiedene Weise mit Grundformen der Gestaltung, Marcel Duchamp thematisierte den Kontext Kunstmuseum, Yves Klein, Barnett Newman und Rupprecht Geiger problematisierten die Farbe, zum Teil in monochromer Art, Lucio Fontana die Leinwand, Andy Warhol Original und Iteration, Donald Judd die Hängung und Cy Twombly die Spur. Und ganz zum Schluss, quasi am Ende der Avantgardezeit, blieb noch das Konzept, die Idee. Heinz Gappmayr, Sol LeWitt, Robert Barry, Joseph Kosuth, Lawrence Weiner, Hanne Darboven waren hier die großen Vertreter in den 60er und 70er Jahren des letzten Jahrhunderts. Berühmt wurden die drei Möglichkeitsformen künstlerischer Praxis von Lawrence Weiner: 1. Der Künstler kann die Arbeit machen, 2. die Arbeit kann von einer anderen Person hergestellt werden, 3. die Arbeit muss nicht realisiert werden.

Diese Vergeistigung der Kunst ging einher mit einer Aufwertung des Rezipienten. Wenn Heinz Gappmayr zu einer Ausstellung mit dem Titel »Linie« eingeladen hatte, und man in einen weißen leeren Raum geführt wurde und man nach einigem Suchen in der Mitte des Raumes am Boden einen kleinen schwarzen Kreis sah und dann entdeckte, dass im rechten Winkel an der Decke ebenso ein kleiner schwarzer Kreis war, dann war die Linie zwischen diesen beiden Punkten eben bloß als gedachte im Kopf des jeweiligen Rezipienten.

Die Dokumenta 6 1977 von Manfred Schneckenburger wurde von der Konzeptkunst dominiert. Sie war von der Tendenz schwarz/weiß, eben wie der Name Konzept schon sagt, mehr geistig als sinnlich. Viele Kunstkenner dachten damals, jetzt hat sich die Kunst in Geist aufgelöst, was soll denn jetzt noch kommen? Wie es weiterging ist bekannt, Postavantgarde, Postmoderne, Neue Wilde waren die Schlagworte danach, die Farbe, die Expression, das Abbild waren wieder da und die alten orthodoxen Avantgardisten waren höchst verunsichert von all diesen Tendenzen, die sie letztlich für überflüssig hielten, denn für sie waren das ja alte Hüte. So entstand der Vorwurf postmoderner Beliebigkeit, während die Apologeten der Postmoderne vom Stilpluralismus, der Mehrfachcodierung und der Ironie schwärmten. Heute 2014 will niemand mehr zur Postmoderne gezählt werden, entweder man spricht wieder von der Moderne oder im Sinne von Heinrich Klotz und Ulrich Beck von der Zweiten Moderne.

Dieser Schnelldurchgang durch die Geschichte der Moderne wurde fokussiert auf ein paar wenige Eckpunkte, die dazu beitragen, die Relevanz der künstlerischen Arbeiten Armin Lindauers und ihre Verortung in der Kunstgeschichte zu begreifen. Sofort ins Auge fällt der Abbildcharakter, die malerische Farbigkeit und die Größe der Arbeiten Lindauers. Hier wurde nicht an Sinnlichkeit gespart, weder visuell noch olfaktorisch. Das Terpentin der Ölfarbe, den Geruch des Malerateliers, hat man in der Nase, wenn man diese Bilder betrachtet – nicht umsonst wurden Maler, durchaus nicht abwertend gemeint, gerne als Malschweine bezeichnet. Kein Wunder, dass diese ausgeprägte Sinnlichkeit zur Lust der Betrachtung beim Rezipienten führt.

Interessant ist nun, dass Lindauers Arbeiten satter Sinnlichkeit sehr wohl die alte Frage Cézannes, »was ist ein Bild«, thematisieren. Dies geschieht aber ohne das Abbild aufzugeben, ohne abstrakt zu werden und ohne in die Vergeistigung und damit in die Entsinnlichung der alten Konzeptkunst der 60er und 70er Jahre des letzten Jahrhunderts zu fallen. Lindauer zeigt reflexive Kunst mit malerischen Mitteln. Was passiert, wenn die Bildgrenze, der Rahmen, selbst zum Bild, zur Malerei, wird? Wie ist die Dialektik von Gezeigtem und Nichtgezeigtem, wenn nur gemalte Rahmenausschnitte präsentiert werden? Wie ist das Verhältnis von Figur und Grund und auf welche Weisen kann das Abbild an die Sinngrenze getrieben werden? Lindauer stellt nicht die Frage nach den Bedingungen der Möglichkeit des Bildes, denn dies würde in die Transzendentalphilosophie der logischen Bildbedingungen führen, sondern fragt nach den sinnlichen und malerischen Bedingungen des Bildes.

Er bleibt damit im kantschen Reich der empirisch-sinnlichen Notwendigkeit, was dazu führt, dass die oben genannte dritte von Lawrence Weiner genannte Möglichkeit künstlerische Praxis, eine Arbeit müsse nicht realisiert werden (denn es genüge die bloße Formulierung der Idee), bei Lindauers Art der Konzeptkunst nicht möglich ist. Die jeweilige sinnliche Realisierung ist notwendiger Bestandteil und führt zu einer Repotenzierung des Künstlers und seiner Produktion.

Eine berühmte Serie von Arbeiten, die der Kozeptkünstler Joseph Kosuth im Jahr 1965 erstellt hat, hieß One and three saws, hammers, chairs, boxes, brooms usw. Sie wurde der Tatsache gerecht, dass das Medium Fotografie, wie oben schon vermerkt, materialistischer Motor für das Reflexivwerden der Kunst war. Kosuth präsentiert in dieser Serie jeweils einen Gegenstand dreimal. Einmal als reales Ding, zum Beispiel eine Säge, links davon hängt die Schwarzweißfotografie dieser Säge, und rechts davon ein Lexikonartikel zum Begriff Säge. Die Säge erscheint dreifach als Ding, Fotografie und Begriff. Farbe hat hier keine Relevanz. Anders bei Lindauer, er spielt die Verhältnisse von Ding, Fotografie und Malerei durch. Dann wird die Farbe wichtig, nicht nur als gemalte, sondern auch als (Farb-)Fotografie. Das Verhältnis von Malerei und Fotografie organisiert Lindauer dialektisch mit fotografierter Malerei, wie zum Beispiel bei Landschaft mit Feld und Bäumen und mit gemalter Fotografie, wie zum Beispiel bei der Arbeit Diafilmbild. Doch nicht nur das. Bei der Serie Anbetung haben wir den Teppich als reales Ding auf dem Boden liegend und an der Wand hängend als mit Öl gemaltes Bild in vergrößerter Form. Hier soll man nicht nur denkend über die Differenz von realem Ding und Abbild reflektieren, wie bei Kosuth, sondern als Rezipient ist man aufgefordert leibhaftig die Aneignung der Arbeit zu leisten, durch das Niederknien auf dem Teppich. Durch die Adoration wird der aufrechte Gang des Rezipienten aufgegeben, was wunderbar die Ambivalenz der Kunst selbst ausdrückt, denn nicht selten wurde sie unterschätzt und überschätzt zugleich. Sie wurde entweder schlichtweg ignoriert und zugleich im doppelten Sinne überbewertet, die einen witterten bei jeder neuen Kunst den Untergang des Abendlandes und die anderen die Rettung desselben. Bei allen Unterschieden zwischen Kosuth und Lindauer, gibt es eine Gemeinsamkeit. Beide arbeiten in Serien, die jeweils Untersuchungen zu Aspekten der Kunst und Kunstwahrnehmung sind, beide sind nicht nur Künstler, sondern zugleich Kunstforscher.

Für den Philosophen ist es ein Gemeinplatz, dass gegen Verdinglichung nur Reflexion hilft. Auch Armin Lindauer »verflüssigt«, nicht mit geistigen Mitteln wie der Philosoph, sondern mit malerischen Mitteln, das Ding Bild. Er realisiert dies nicht zuletzt durch das Nichtentfernen unbeabsichtigter Spuren des Malprozesses zum Beispiel auf den leeren Flächen der Rahmenbilder und verdeutlicht dadurch das Verhältnis von Absicht und Aleatorik. Das fertige, verdinglichte Bild, erhält dadurch Hinweise seiner Genese; auch ein Bild ist ein Gewordenes und dieses Gewordensein wird durch diese aleatorischen Zeichen der Entstehung sinnlich wahrnehmbar.

# *Painterly Reflexion.*

**Thomas Friedrich** // *teaches Design Theory and Philosophy at the University of Mannheim*

*The artistic Modern Age begins with a new line of questioning, which was established by Cézanne. Before his lifetime, fine artists were occupied for centuries with how to illustrate the world and its parts correctly. Admittedly, there were permanent disputes over what the world and its parts were, exactly, and what was to be understood by »correctly«, but one thing was indubitable, the image was portrayal. As its ideal form we call to mind a Renaissance tableau, Las Meninas by Velázquez for example. And then Cézanne comes, paints Mont Sainte-Victoire almost hundred times and makes it clear to his brother during protracted correspondence that he was no longer concerned with how nature or culture were portrayed correctly, but that he was troubled by the question of what an image actually was.*

*And precisely with this forward-looking questioning a new era was rung in; fine art became reflexive, became philosophical as it were, without using the philosophical medium of theoretical texts but the creative resources themselves. The precedent, the portrayal, the Renaissance tableau flew apart, exploded as a result of analysis, was dismantled into its defining individual parts, was destroyed and overturned simultaneously, to express it in a Hegelian way. That is the shock of the modern. The material engine for this repositioning of fine art was the invention of photography in the 19th century, a medium which was able to portray the world as never before, which led Eugène Delacroix to the spontaneous pronouncement, »painting is dead«.*

*The basis of abstract art was now laid, and a few examples of the analytical results deserve a mention here: Kazimir Malevich, Paul Klee and Piet Mondrian dealt, each in his different way, with basic forms of design; Marcel Duchamp thematized the art museum context; Yves Klein, Barnett Newman and Rupprecht Geiger problematized colour, sometimes in a monochrome manner; Lucio Fontana the canvas, Andy Warhol original and iteration, Donald Judd the hanging and Cy Twombly the trace. And right at the close, virtually at the end of the avant-garde period, the concept, the idea, still remained. Heinz Gappmayr, Sol LeWitt, Robert Barry, Joseph Kosuth, Lawrence Weiner, Hanne Darboven were the great representatives in this context in the 60s and 70s of the last century. Lawrence Weiner's three possible forms of artistic practice became famous: 1. The artist can do the work, 2. The work can be produced by another person, 3. The work does not have to be realized.*

*This intellectualization of art was accompanied by a valorization of the recipient. When Heinz Gappmayr issued invitations to an exhibition bearing the title »Line«, and one was conducted into a white empty space and, after some searching, saw on the floor in the middle of the space a small black circle and then discovered that there was likewise a small black circle in the right angle on the ceiling, then the line between these two points was, precisely, merely a thought in the respective recipient's mind.*

*Documenta 6 in 1977 by Manfred Schneckenburger was dominated by conceptual art. It was of the black/white tendency, precisely as the name concept says, more intellectual then sensual. Many art connoisseurs thought at the time that art had now dissolved into intellect; what was supposed to come next? What happened next is well known, post-avant-garde, post-modern, New Wild were the keywords afterwards; colour, expression, portrayal were back and the old orthodox avant-gardists were extremely unsettled by all these trends, which they ultimately held to be superfluous, as they were after all, for them, old hat. There thus arose the accusation of post-modern arbitrariness, while proponents of the post-modern rhapsodized over pluralism of style, multiple coding and irony. Today, in 2014, nobody wants to be counted among the post-modern any more; either the Modern Age is spoken of again or, along the lines of Heinrich Klotz and Ulrich Beck, the Second Modern Age.*

*This quick tour of the history of the Modern Age has been focused on a handful of corner points which provide assistance in grasping the relevance of Armin Lindauer's artistic works and their location in art history. One is struck immediately by the illustrative nature, painterly chromaticity and size of Lindauer's works. No sensuality has been spared here, either visually or olfactorily. The turpentine of the oil paint, the odour of the painter's studio linger in the nose when one looks at these images – not for nothing have painters, not disparagingly at all, been commonly described as wallowing in paint as pigs wallow in mud. No wonder that this pronounced sensuality leads to the recipient's pleasure in beholding.*

*Now, it is interesting that Lindauer's works of saturated sensuality very likely thematize Cézanne's old question, »what is an image«. However, this occurs without abandoning the portrayal, without becoming abstract and without falling into intellectualization and therefore into the de-sensualizing of the former conceptual art of the 60s and 70s of the last century. Lindauer exhibits reflexive art using painterly means. What happens when the visual limit, the frame, becomes itself an image, a painting? What does the dialectic of shown and not-shown look like when only painted frame clippings are presented? What is the relationship between figure and ground and in what ways can the portrayal be driven to the sensual limit? Lindauer does not pose the question of the image's conditions of possibility, for this would lead into the transcendental philosophy of logical visual conditions, but inquires after the image's sensual and painterly conditions. He therefore remains in the Kantian realm of empirical-sensory necessity, which has the result that the abovementioned third possibility of artistic possibility named by Lawrence Winter, that a work does not have to be realized (for the mere formulation of the idea suffices), is not possible with Lindauer's kind of conceptual art. The respective sensual realization is a necessary component and leads to a repotentization of the artist and his production.*

*A famous series of works, which the conceptual artist Joseph Kosuth created in 1965, was called One and three saws, hammers, chairs, boxes, brooms etc. It acknowledged the fact that the medium of photography, as already noted above, was the material engine for art's becoming reflexive. In this series Kosuth presents one object three times in each case. Once as a real thing, for example a saw; to the left of it hangs the black-and-white photograph of this saw, and to the right a dictionary definition of the term saw. The saw appears three times as a thing, photograph, and concept. Colour has no relevance here. Unlike with Lindauer, he runs through the relationships between thing, photograph, and painting. Colour then becomes important, not only as painted, but also as (colour) photography. Lindauer organizes the relationship between painting and photography dialectically using photographed painting, as for example in Landschaft mit Feld und Bäumen and using painted photography, as for example in the work Diafilmbild. But not only that. With the series Anbetung we have the carpet lying on the floor as a real thing and hanging on the wall as an oil painting in enlarged form. Here, one is expected not only to reflect thoughtfully on the difference between real thing and portrayal, as with Kosuth, but as a recipient one is called on to physically appropriate the work by kneeling down on the carpet. As a result of the adoration the recipient's upright gait is abandoned, which wonderfully expresses the ambivalence of art itself, for not rarely it has been simultaneously undervalued and overvalued. Art has been either simply ignored and simultaneously overrated in the double sense; with each new art form, some sensed the Western world's downfall and others the salvation of the same. For all the differences between Kosuth and Lindauer, there is one common point. Both work in series, which are each investigations on aspects of art and perception of art; both are not only artists, but art researchers at the same time.*

*For the philosopher it is a commonplace that only reflexion provides a remedy against objectification. Armin Lindauer, too, »liquefies«, not using intellectual resources as does the philosopher, but using painterly means, the thing called image. He realizes this not least through the non-elimination of unintended traces of the painting process, on the blank surfaces of the framed pictures for example, and thereby illustrates the relationship between intention and aleatorics. The finished, objectified image obtains, through this, hints as to its genesis; even an image is something that has become and this state of having become is made perceptible through the senses by these aleatory signs of arising.*

**Findling / *Foundling***
Blechdose / *tin can*
13 x 10 cm · 2017

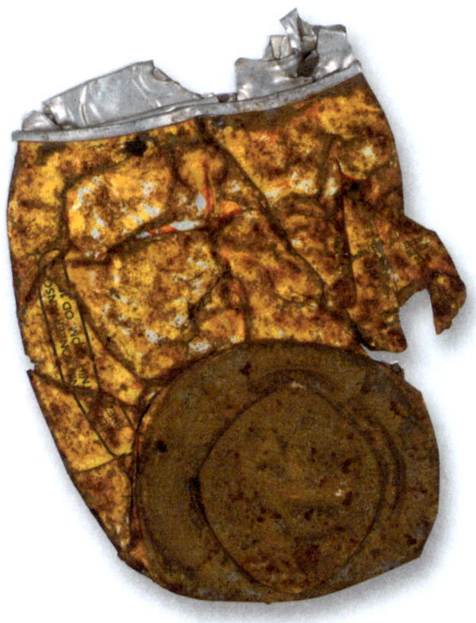

Findling
*Foundling*
2016

Manche Bilder haben mehrere,
sich auch widersprechende Logiken,
die zusammen trotzdem richtig sind.
*Some images have several,
even self-contradictory logics which together,
nevertheless, are right.*

**Rahmenbild** / ***Frame picture***
Öl auf Nessel / *Oil on nettle cloth*
180 x 145 cm · 2015/2017

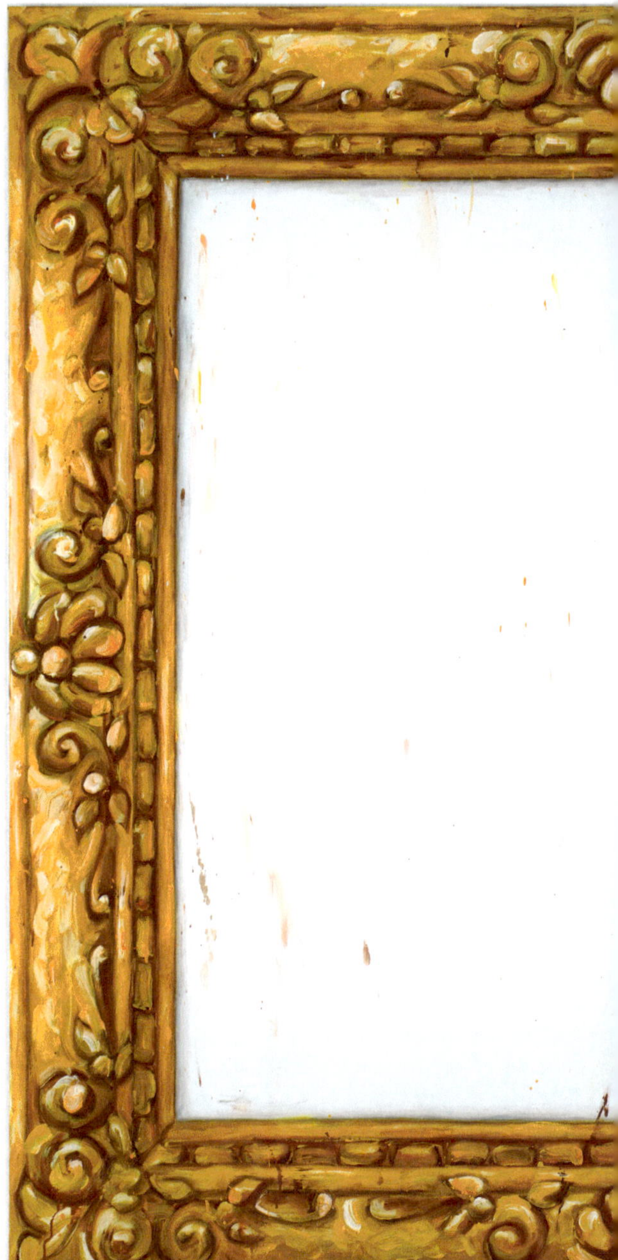

**Rahmenbild / *Frame picture***
Triptychon / *Triptych*
Öl auf Leinwand / *Oil on canvas*
je / *each* 180 x 90 cm · 2015

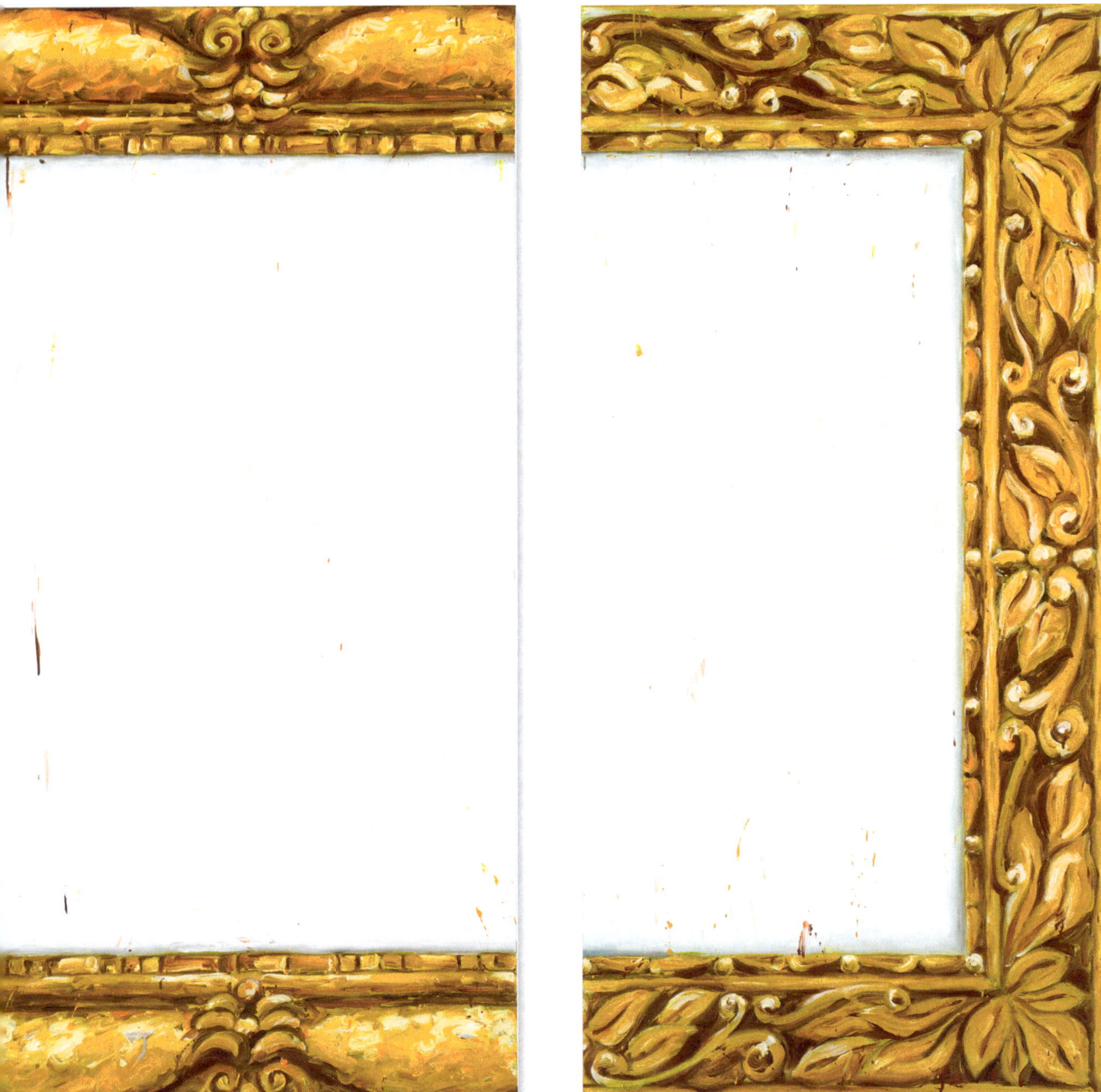

**Rahmenbild / *Frame picture***
Öl auf Leinwand / *Oil on canvas*
130 x 180 cm · 2013

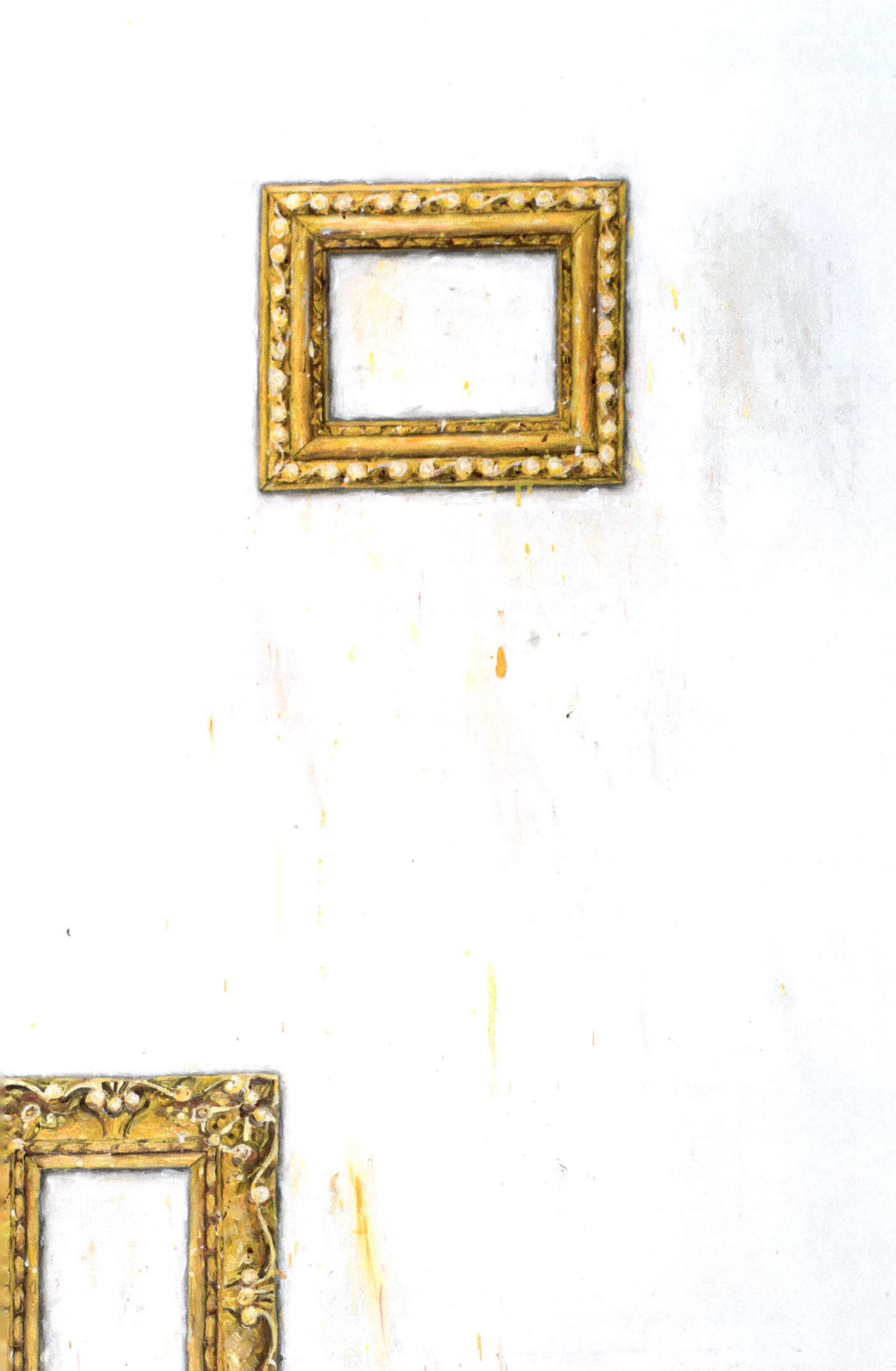

Der Fehler beginnt nicht damit,
»dass einer sich anschickt, Keilrahmen und Leinwand zu kaufen«.
Der Fehler beginnt damit, an Fehler zu glauben.
*The mistake begins not in buying stretch frame and canvas.*
*The mistake begins in believing in mistakes.*

**Rahmenbild / *Frame picture***
Öl auf Leinwand, Goldrahmen / *Oil on canvas, Gold frame*
120 x 150 cm · 2013

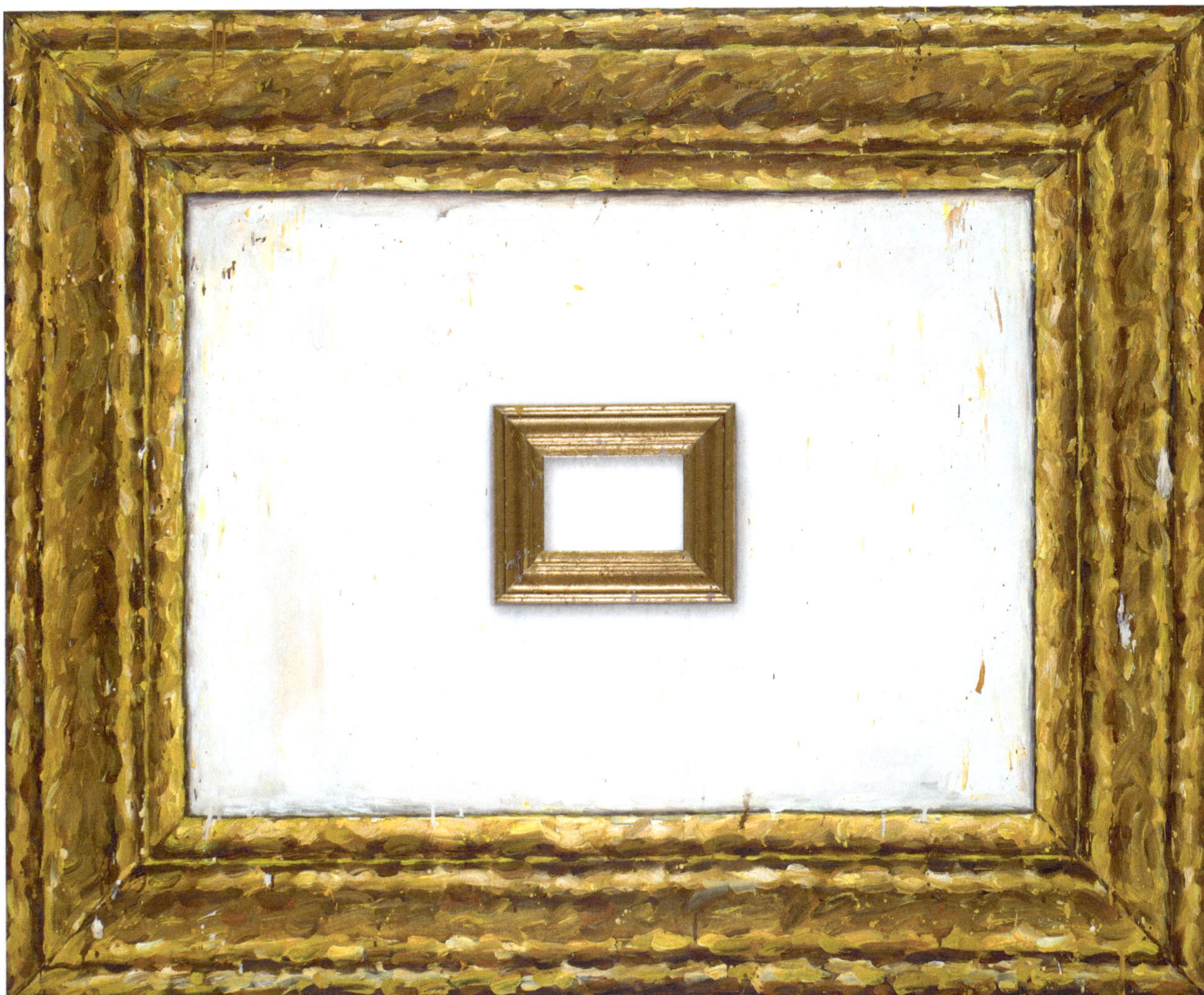

**Rahmenbild / *Frame picture***
Öl auf Leinwand / *Oil on canvas*
60 x 80 cm · 2015

Damit die Bilder gut werden, muss man den Zufall einarbeiten.
*To make the images good, you have to work chance into them.*

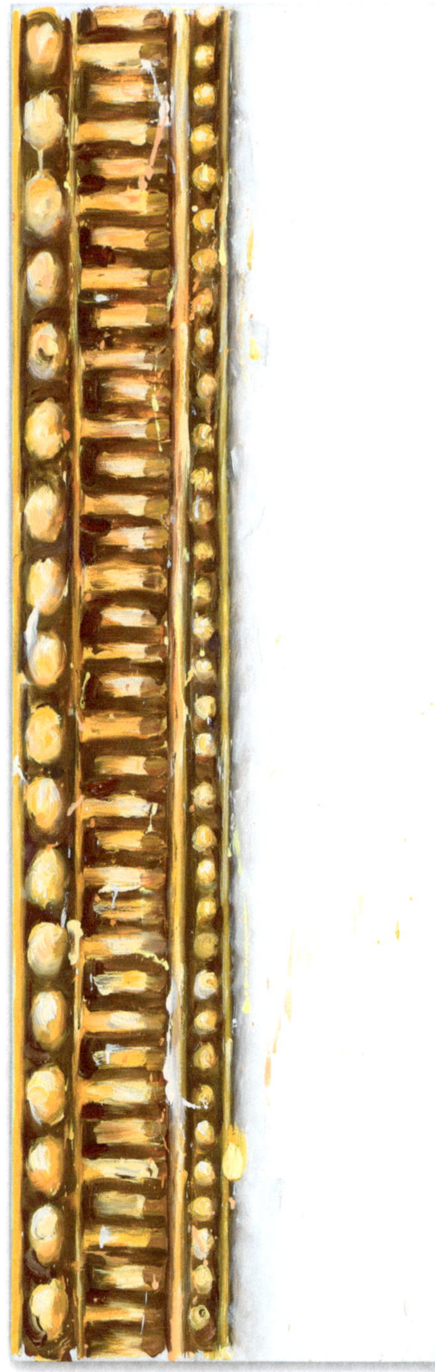

Rahmenbild mit Austern
*Frame picture with oysters*
Öl auf Nessel / *Oil on nettle cloth*
110 x 150,5 cm · 2016/2017

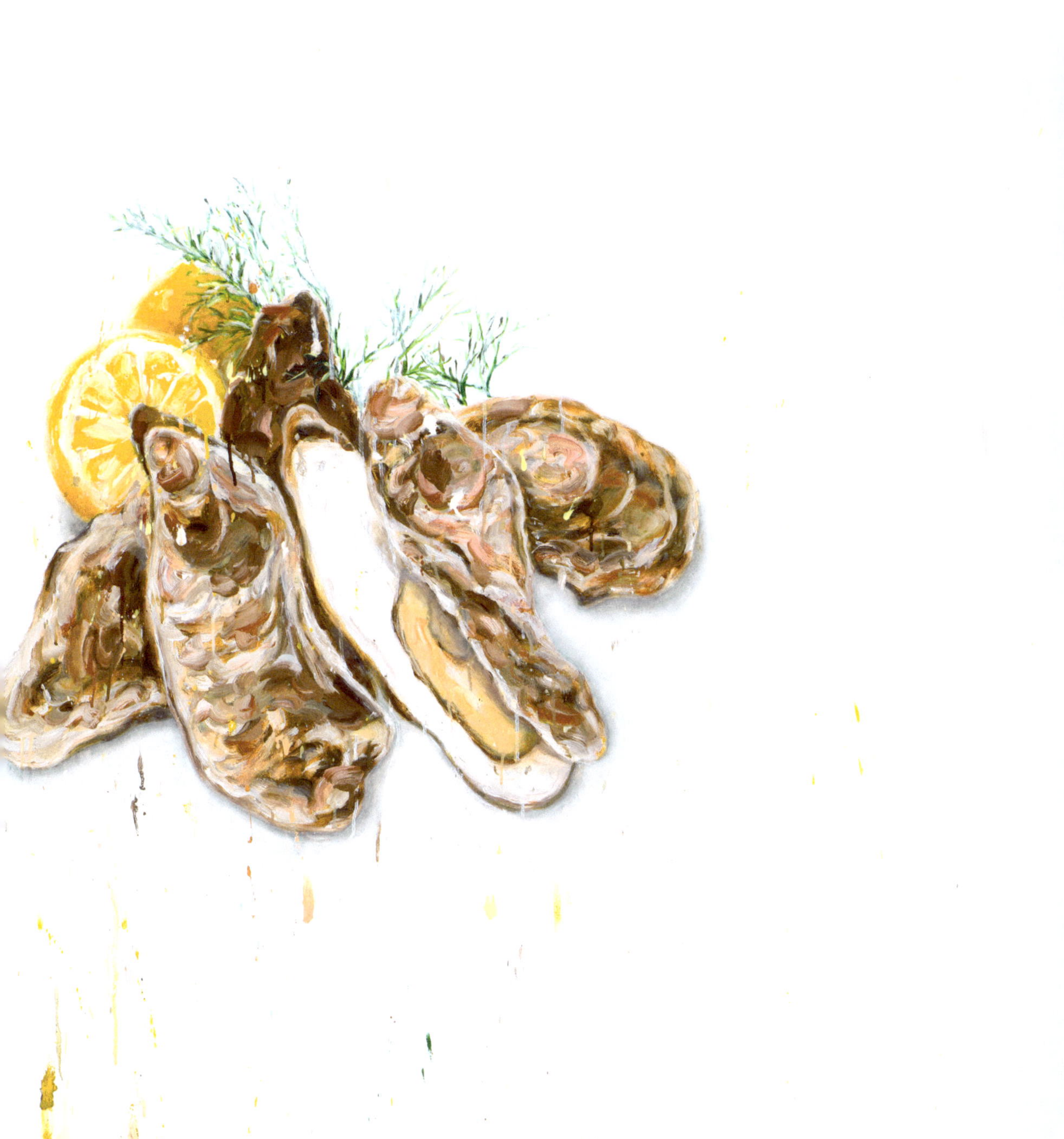

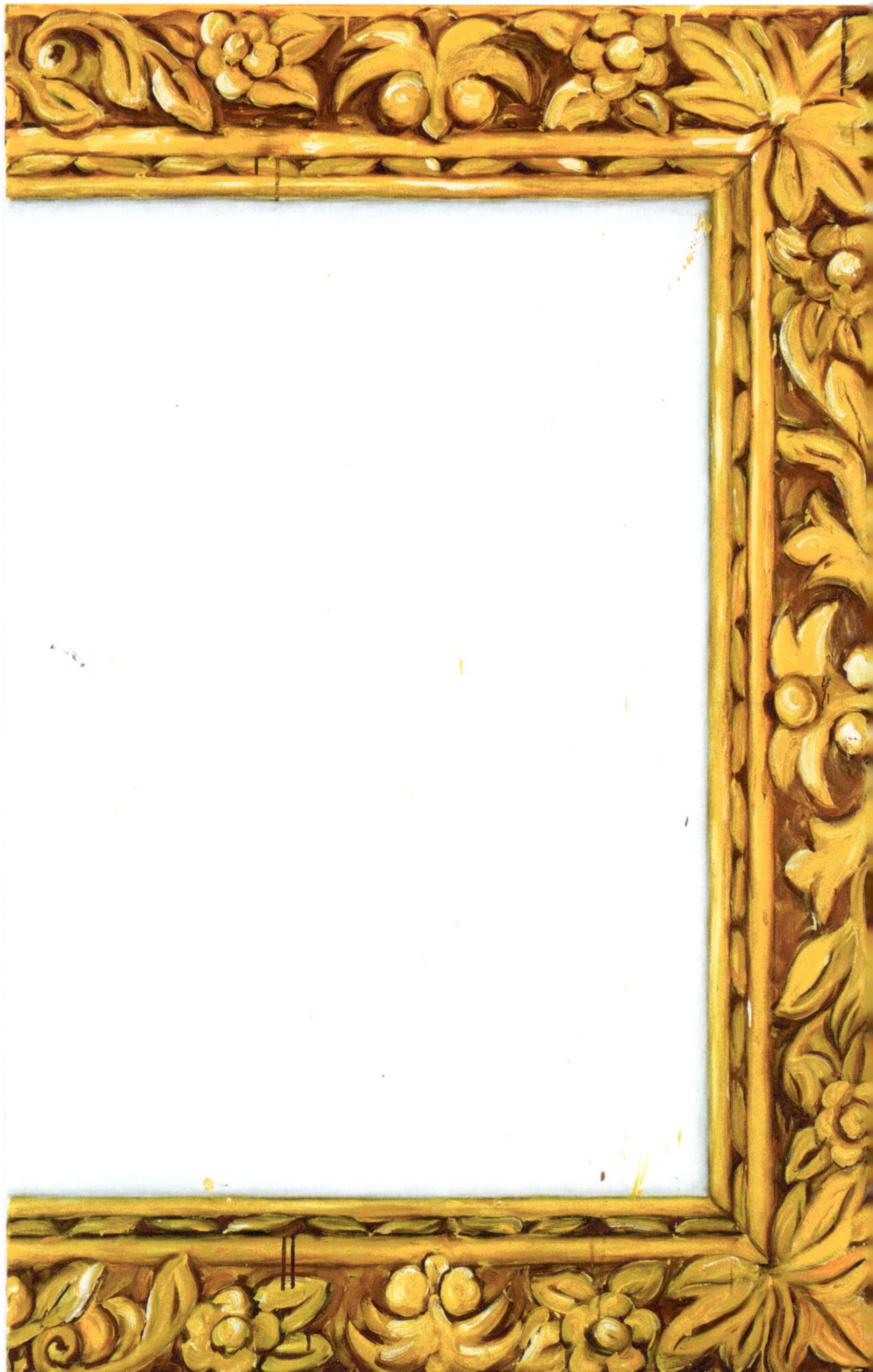

**Rahmenbild / *Frame picture***
Diptychon / *Diptych*
Öl auf Leinwand / *Oil on canvas*
je / *each* 180 x 120 cm · 2015

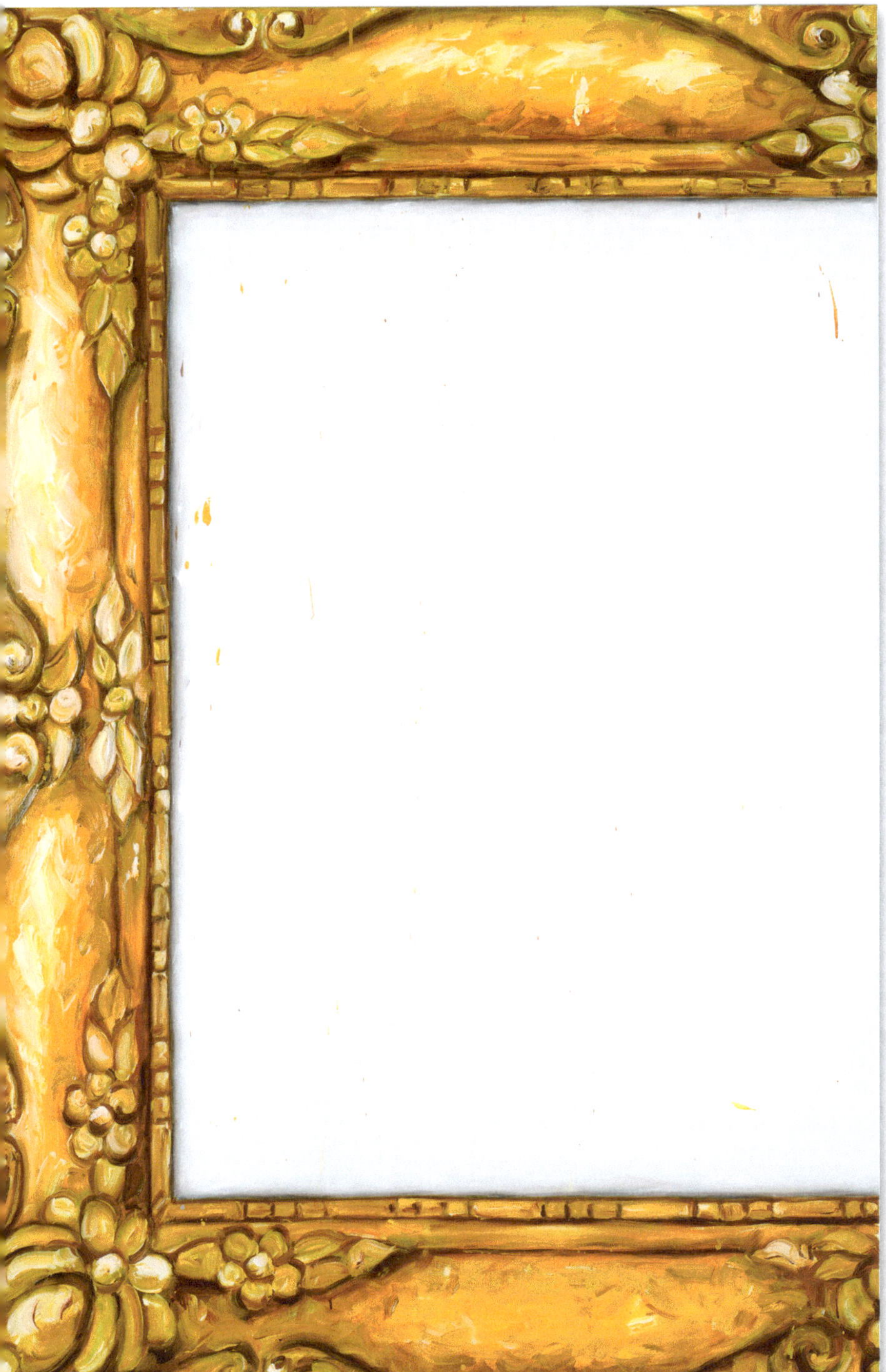

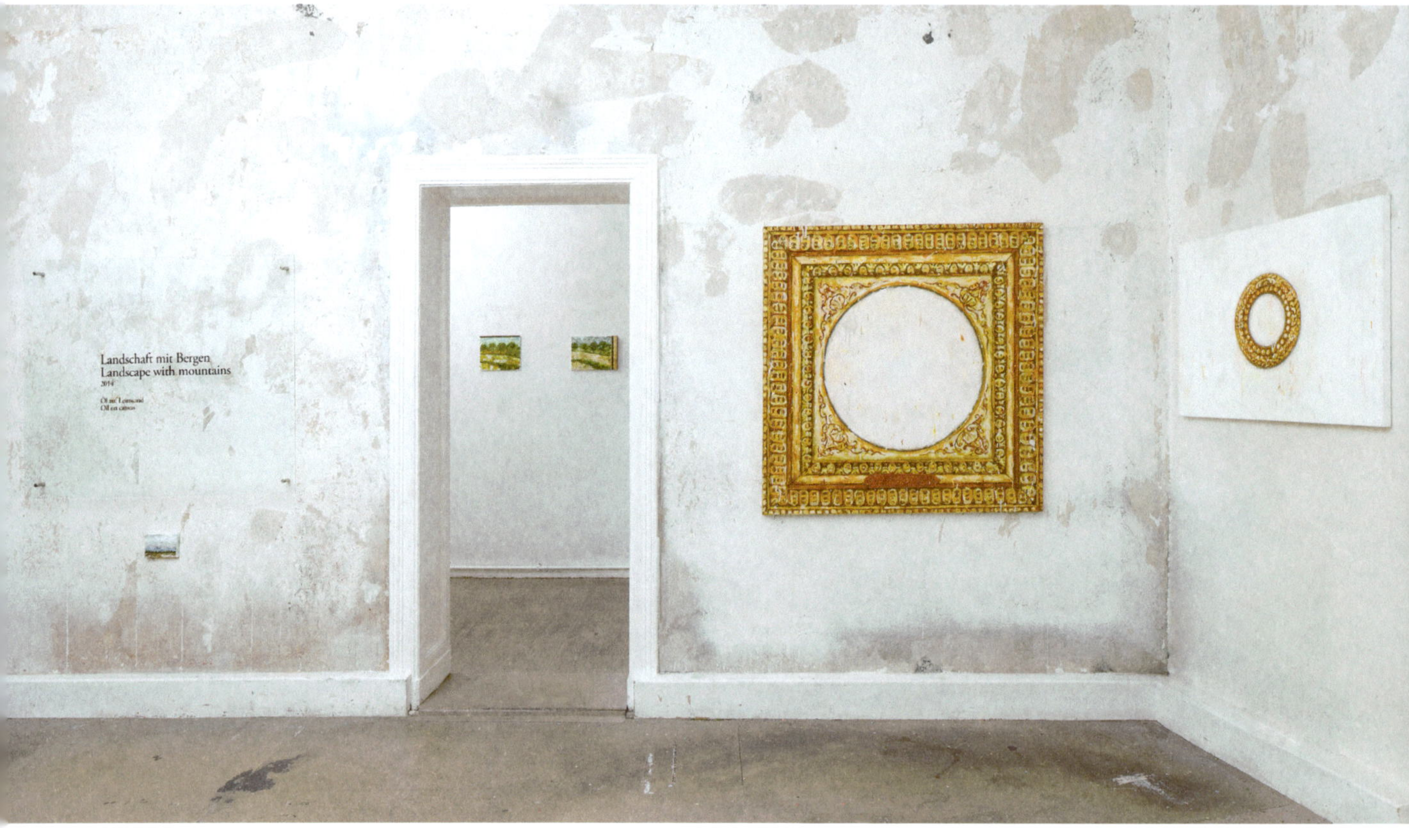
Landschaft mit Bergen
Landscape with mountains

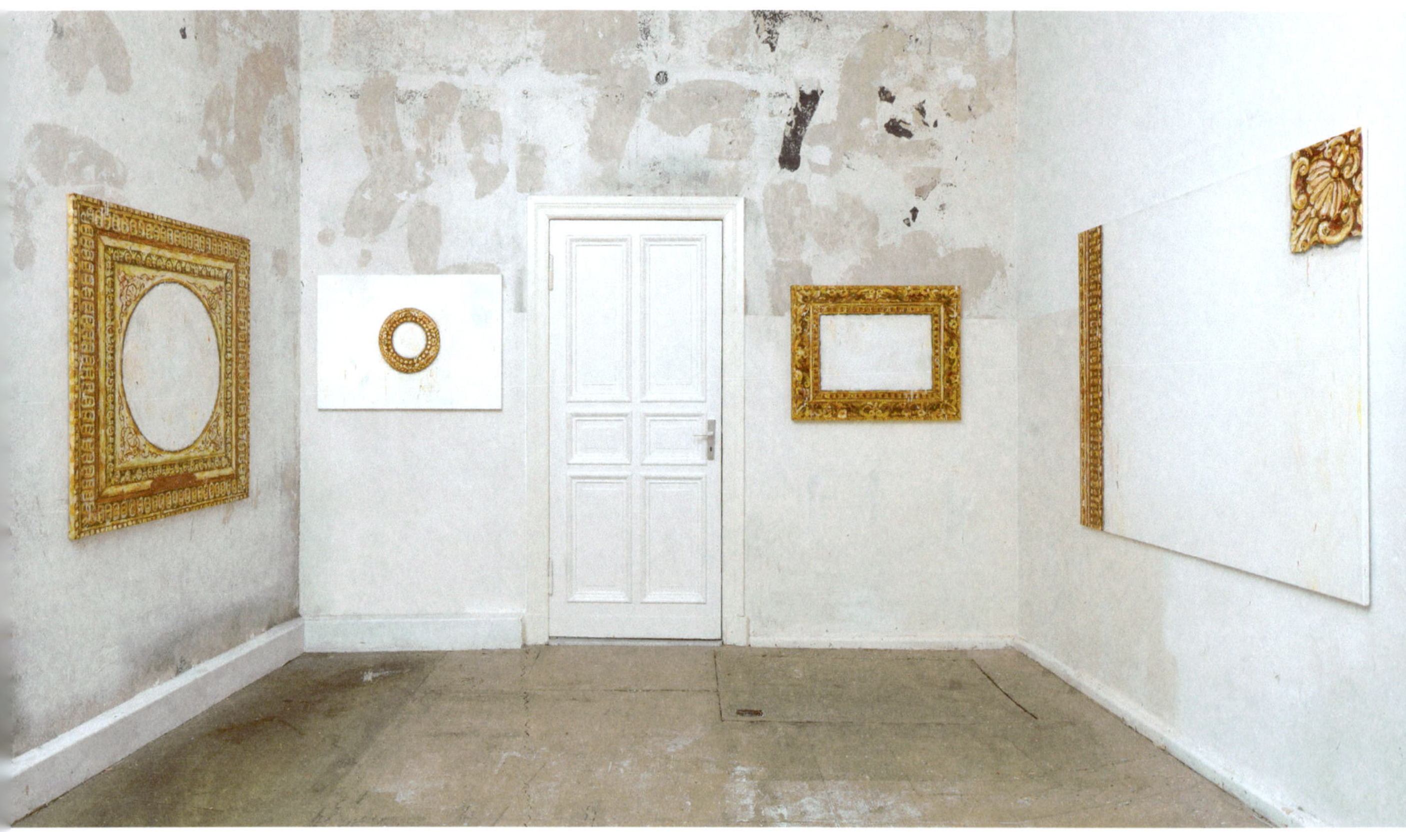

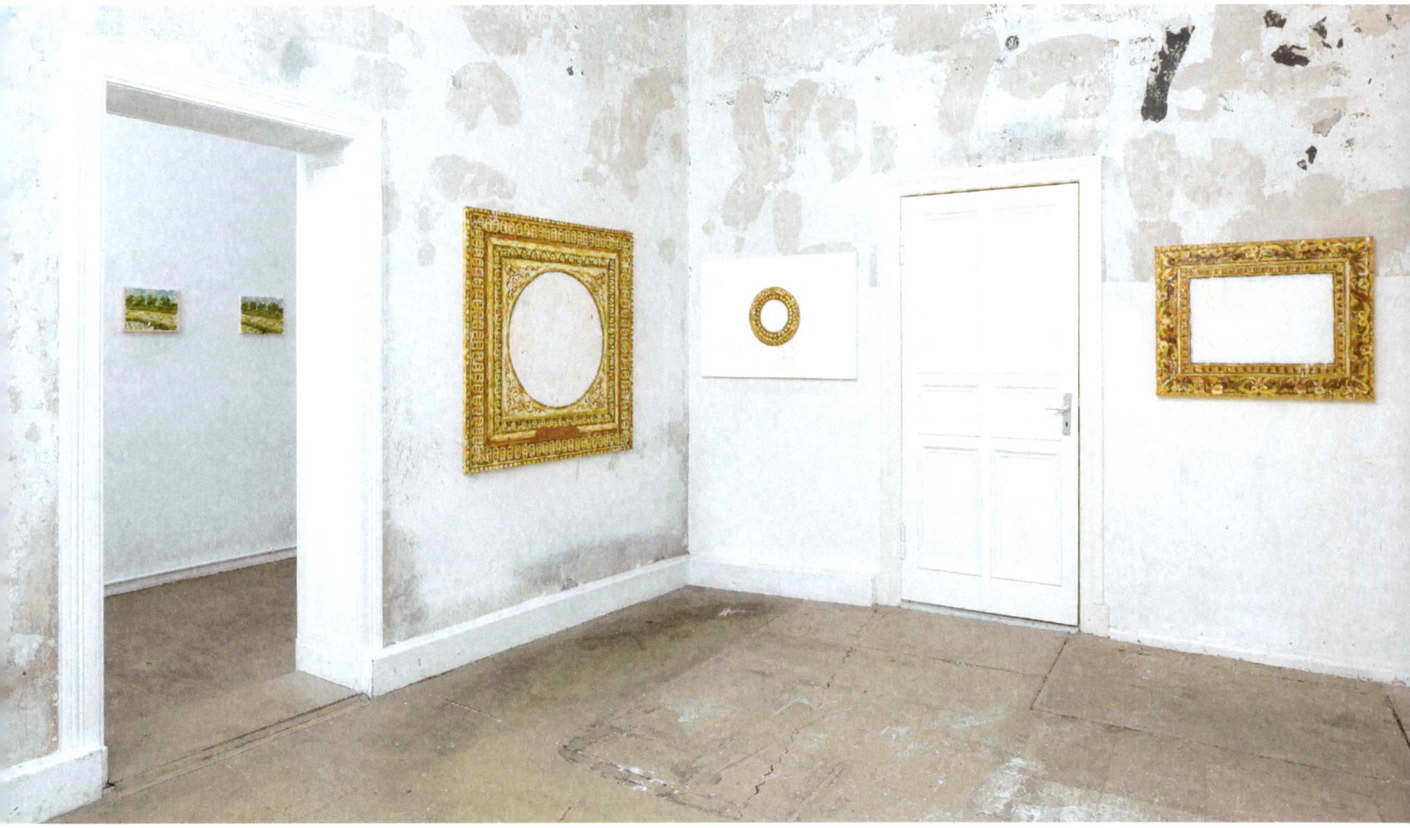

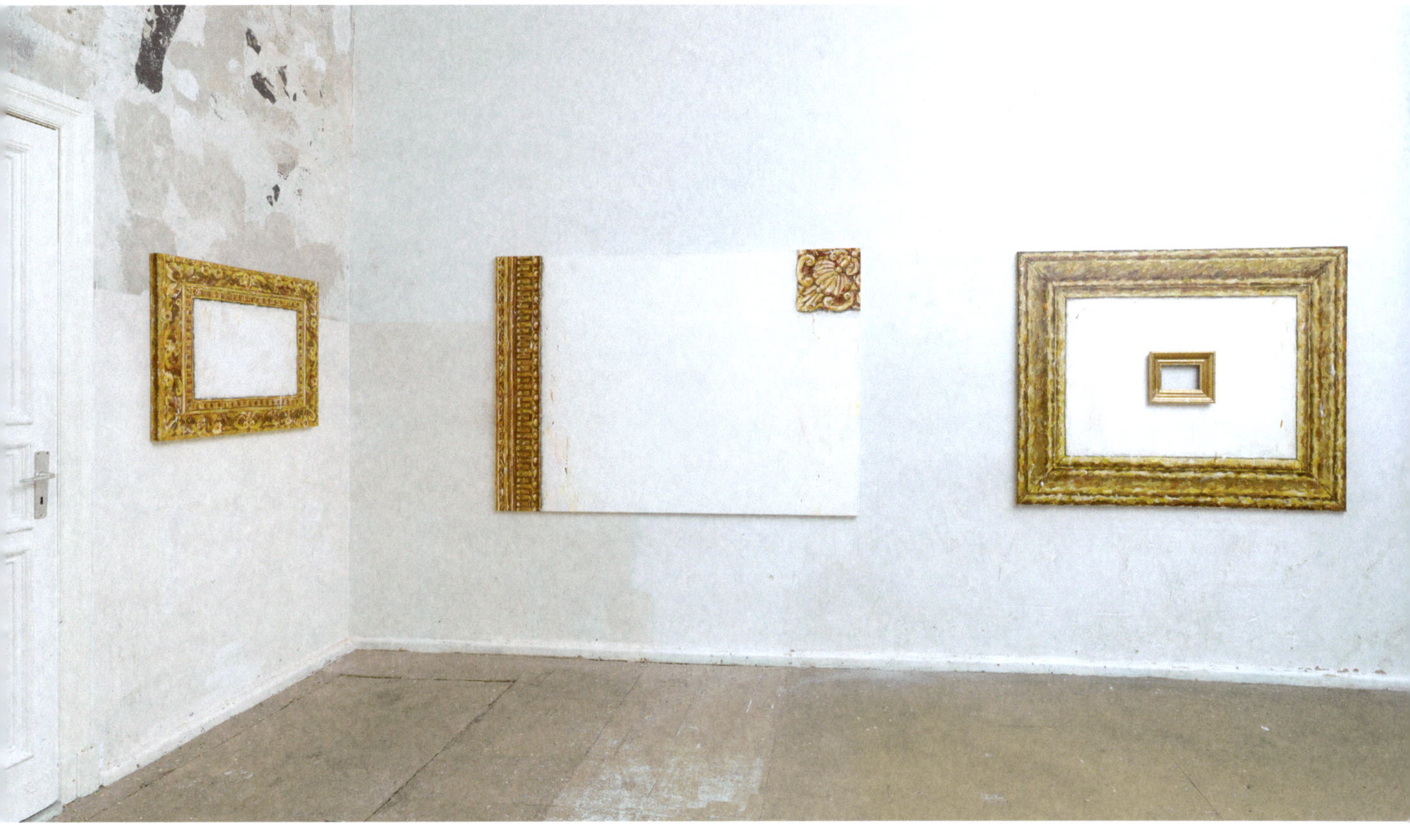

:in Bild ist kein Bild ist ein Bild«, Galerie Z, Berlin, Ausstellungsansicht / *»A picture is no picture is a picture«, Galerie Z, Berlin, Exhibition view*

Eigentlich ist ein abstraktes Bild viel realer als eines, das versucht, die Realität abzubilden.
*In fact an abstract image is more real than one that tries depicting reality.*

**Landschaft mit Weg / *Landscape with path***
Fotodruck auf Alu Dibond / *Fotoprint on Alu Dibond* · 120 x 180 cm
Öl auf Leinwand / *Oil on canvas* · 10 x 15 cm
2014

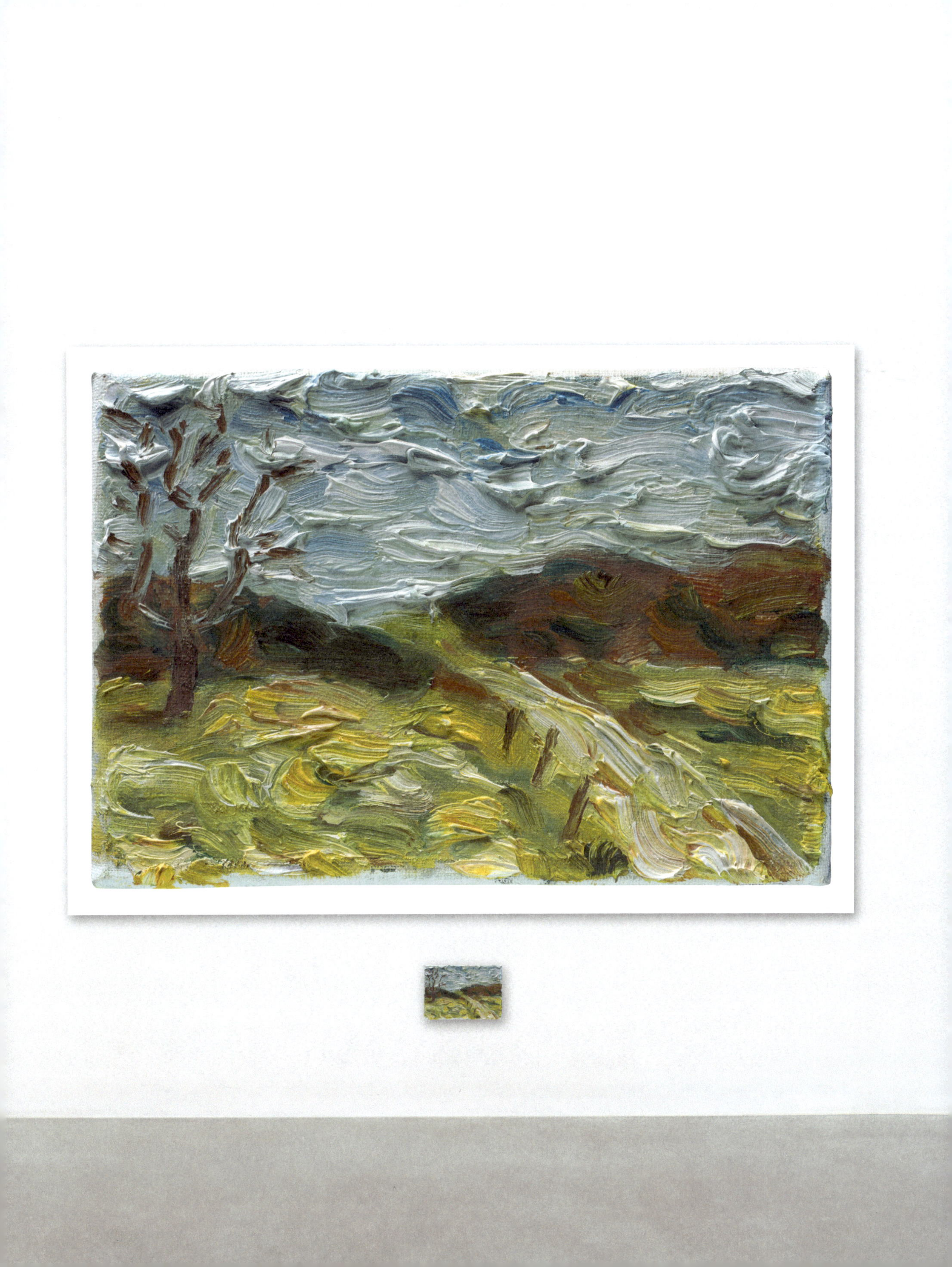

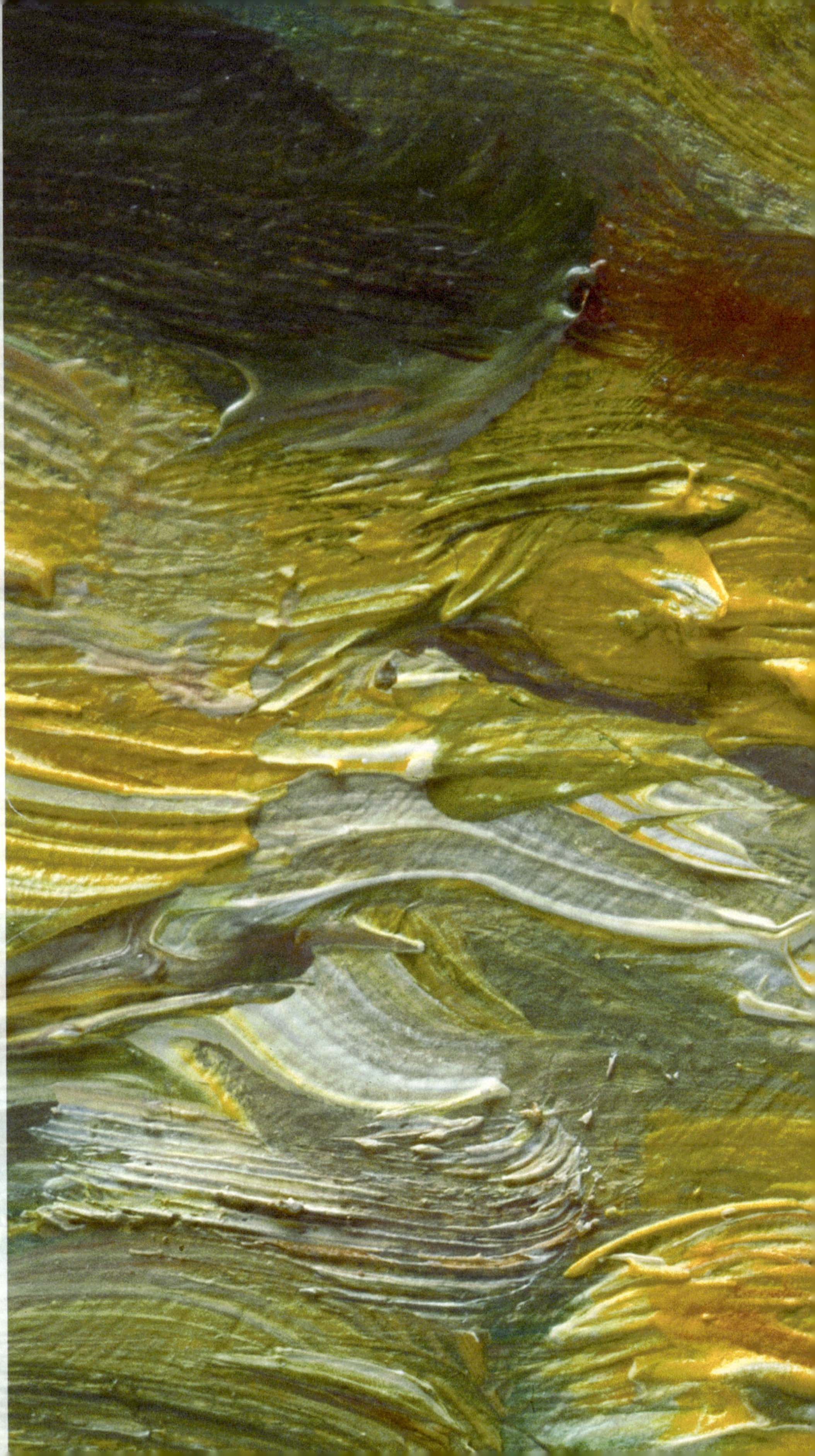

**Landschaft mit Weg** / ***Landscape with path***
Detail (nicht Originalgröße) / *detail (not original size)*

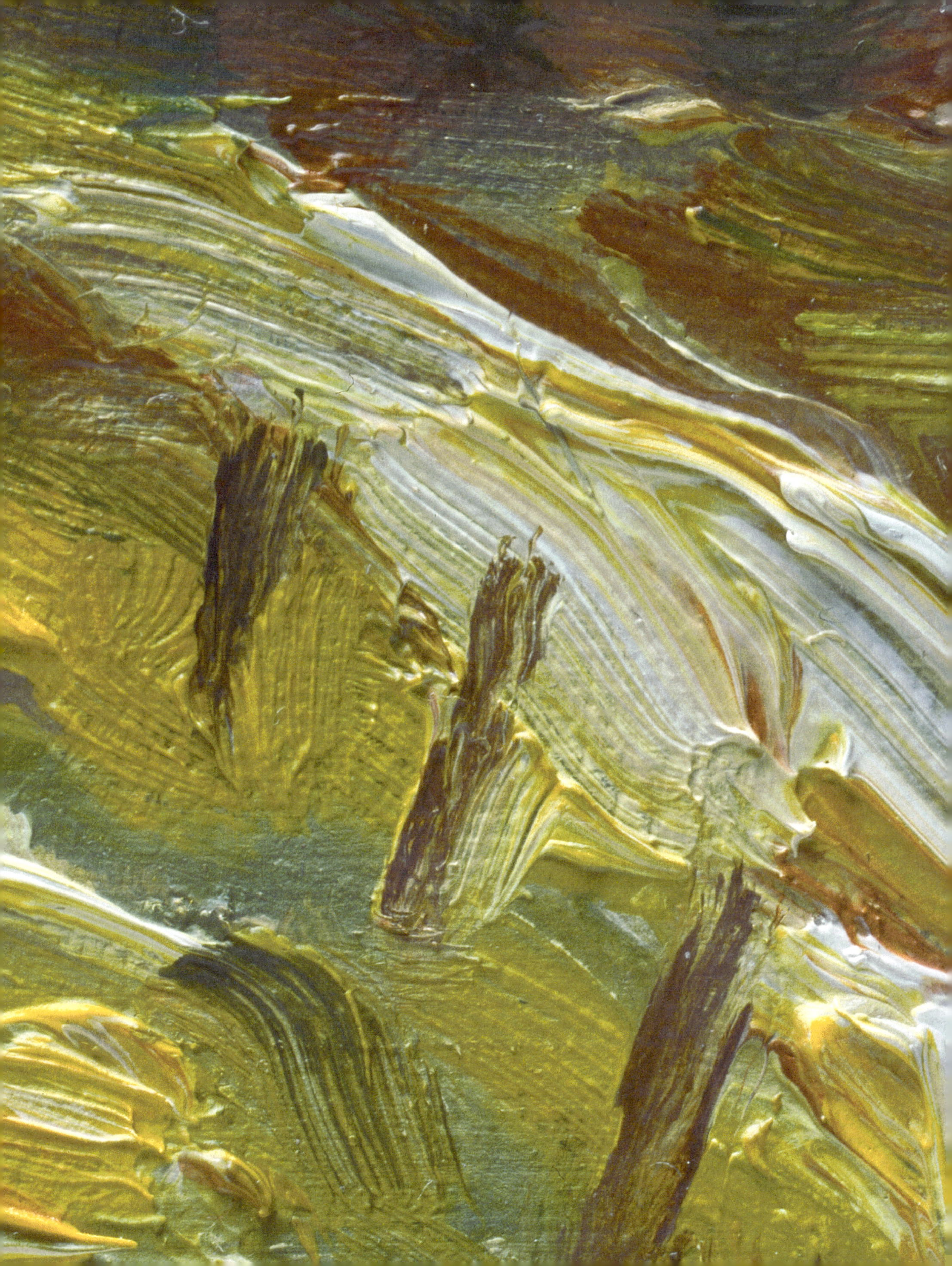

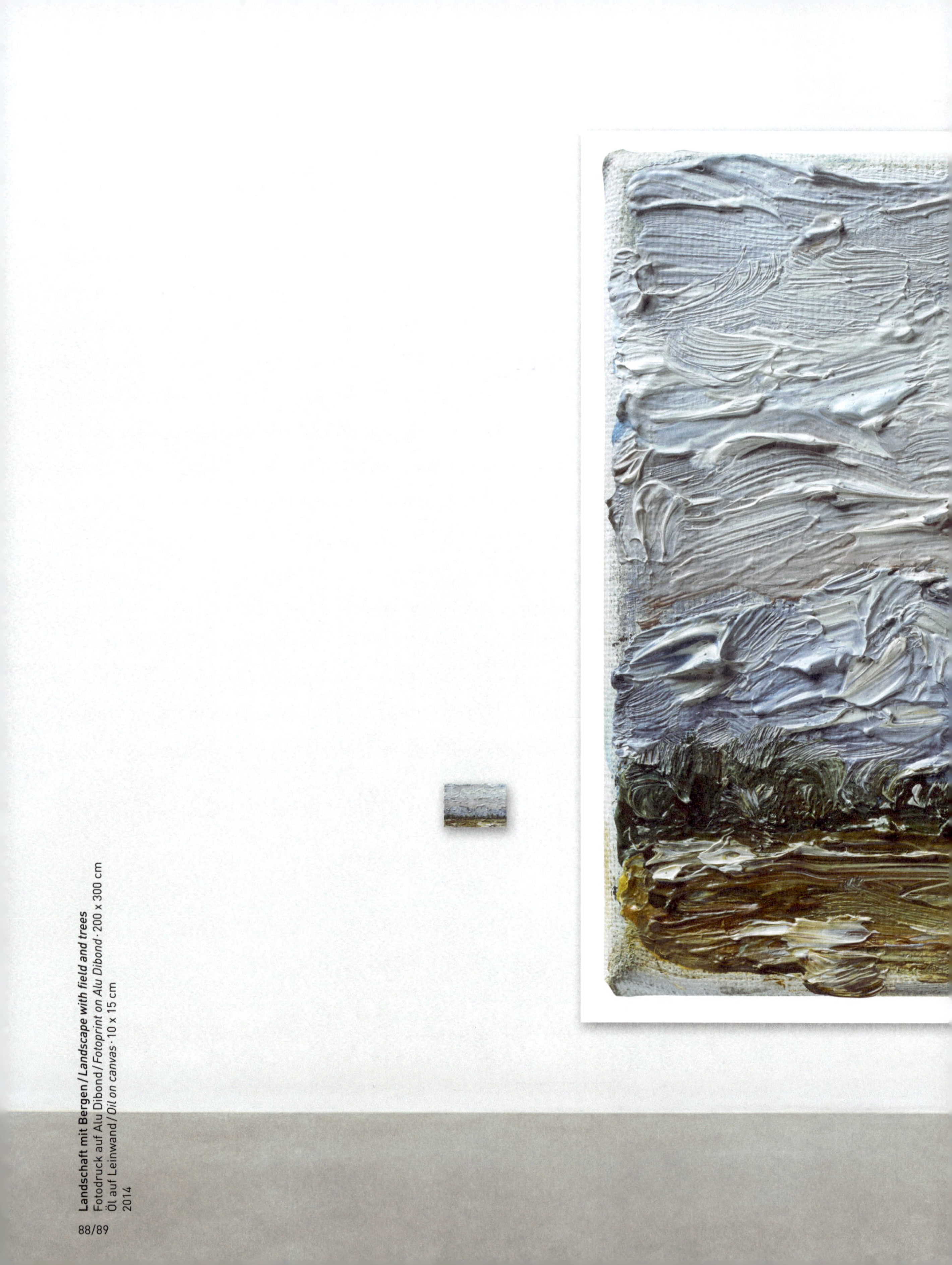

**Landschaft mit Bergen / *Landscape with field and trees***
Fotodruck auf Alu Dibond / *Fotoprint on Alu Dibond* · 200 x 300 cm
Öl auf Leinwand / *Oil on canvas* · 10 x 15 cm
2014

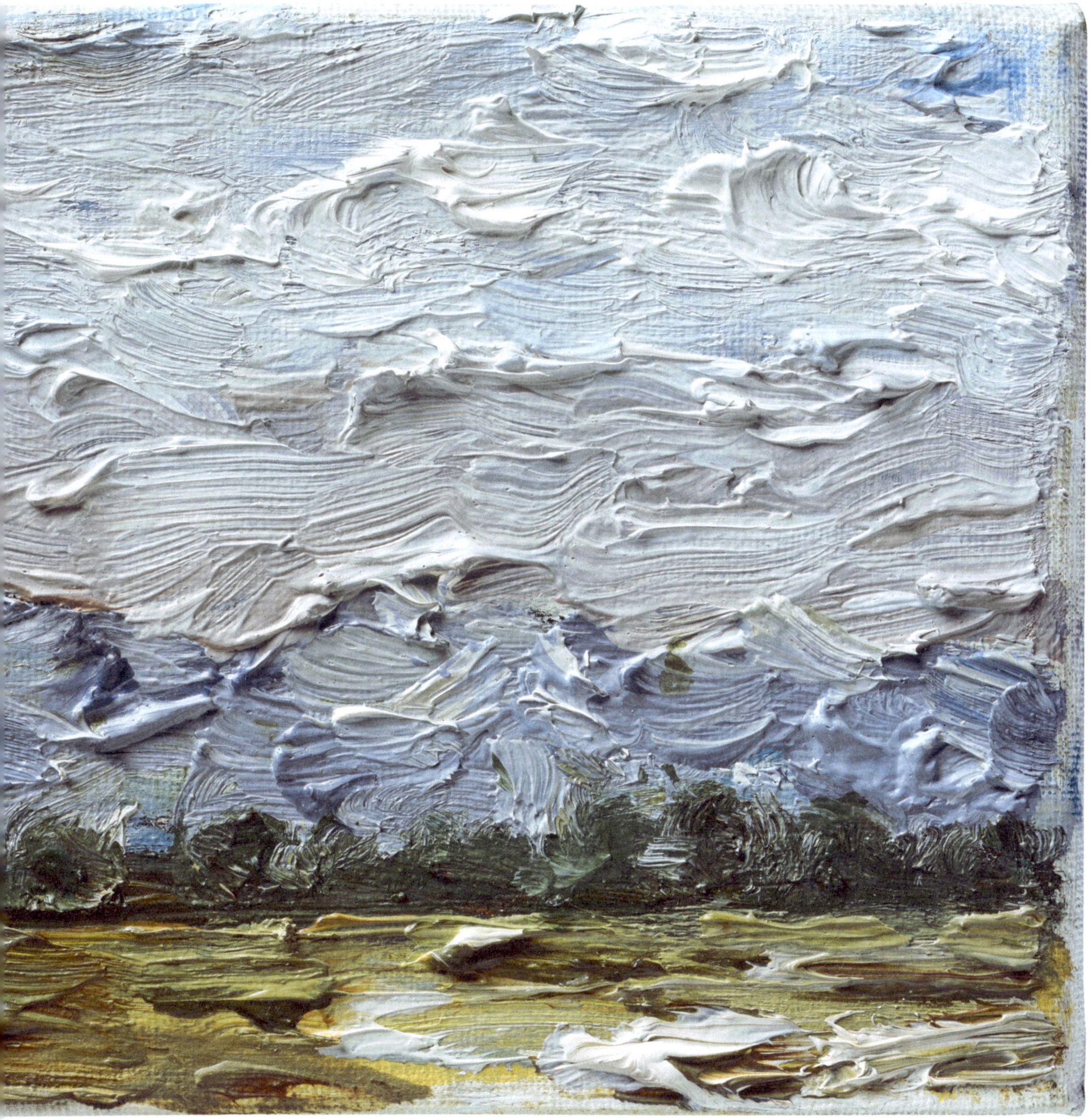

Vielleicht gelingt es, den Betrachter zu verwirren – das wäre ein Erfolg.
*Maybe it will manage to confuse the beholder – that would be a success.*

**Die Büchse der Pandora** / ***Pandora's Box***
Malkasten / *Paintbox* 19,5 x 34 cm
11 Bilder / *11 pictures* 10 x 15 cm · 2018

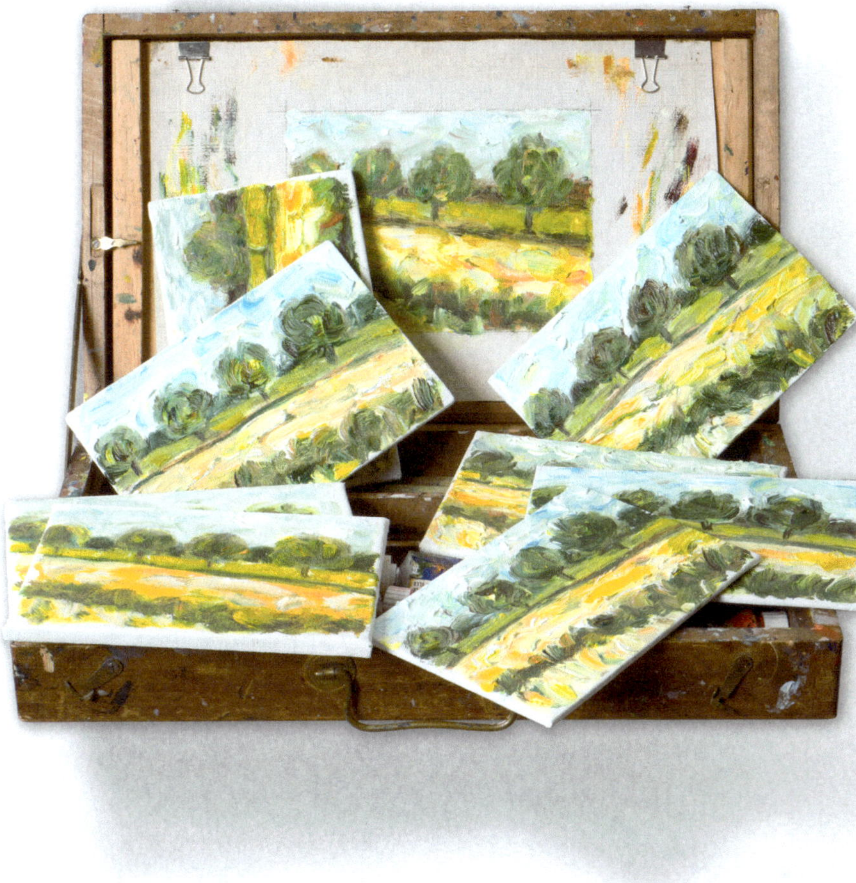

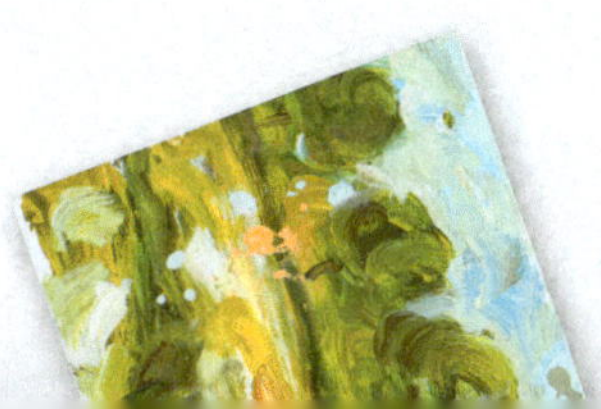

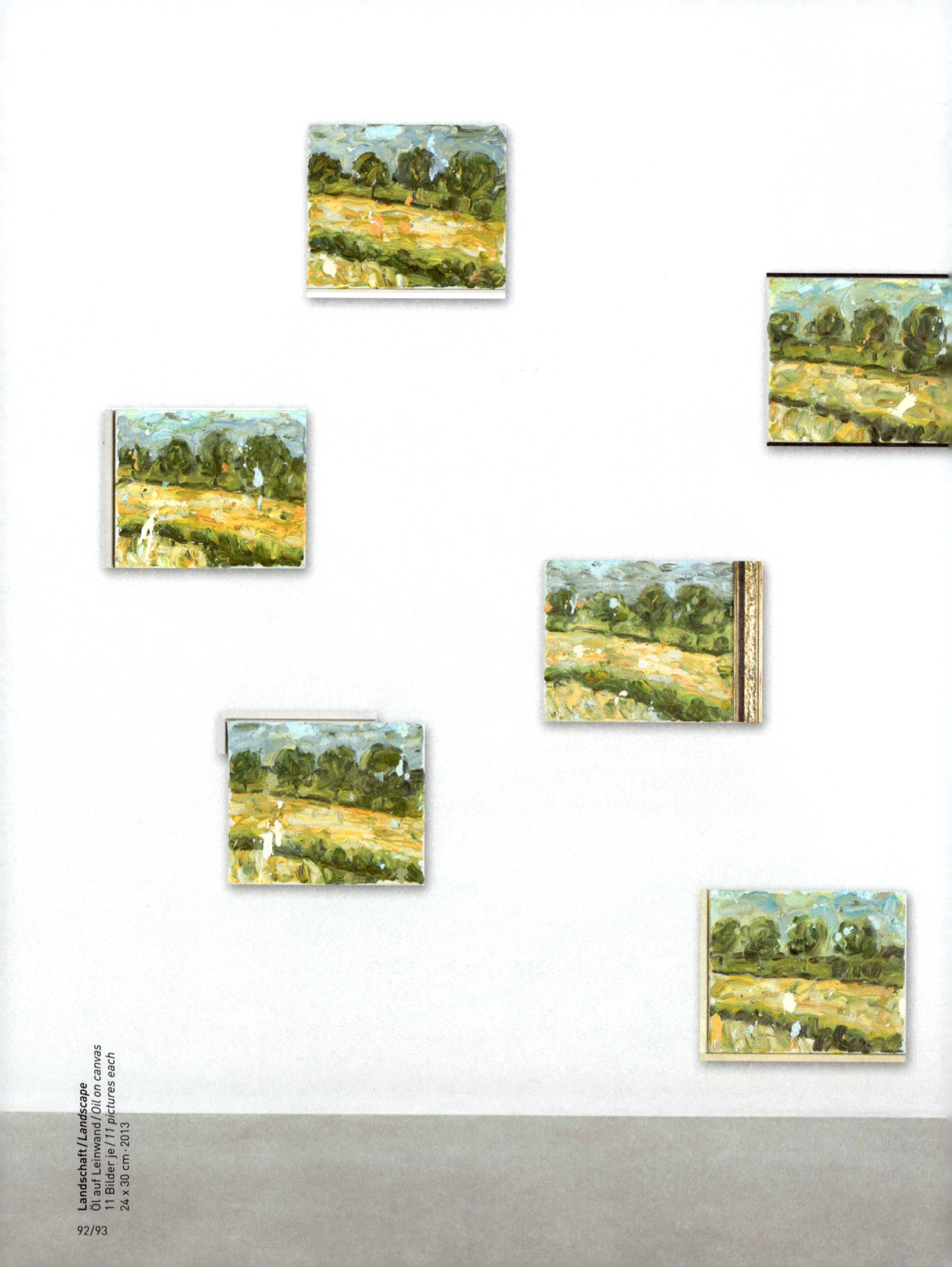

**Landschaft / *Landscape***
Öl auf Leinwand / *Oil on canvas*
11 Bilder je / *11 pictures each*
24 x 30 cm · 2013

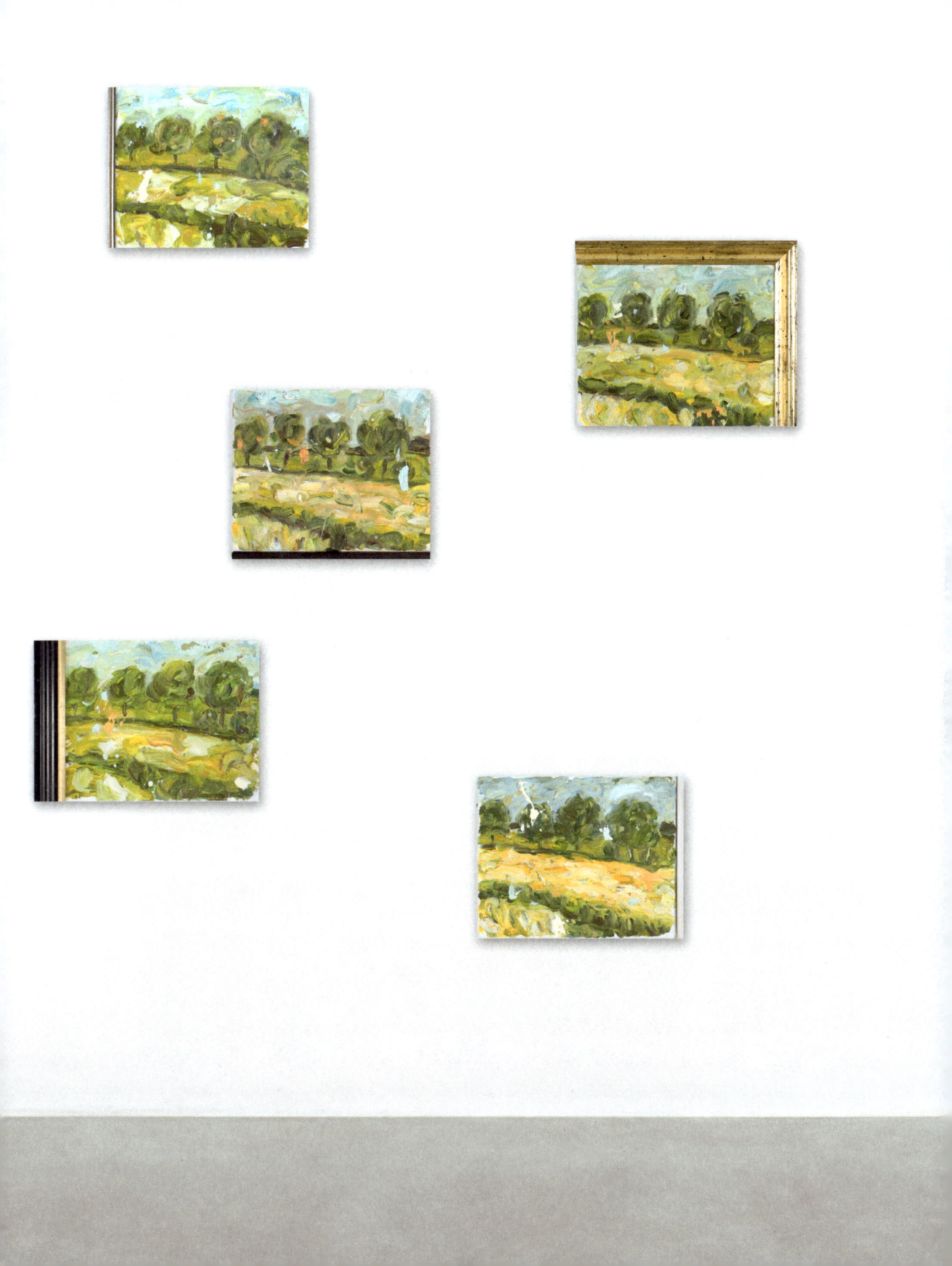

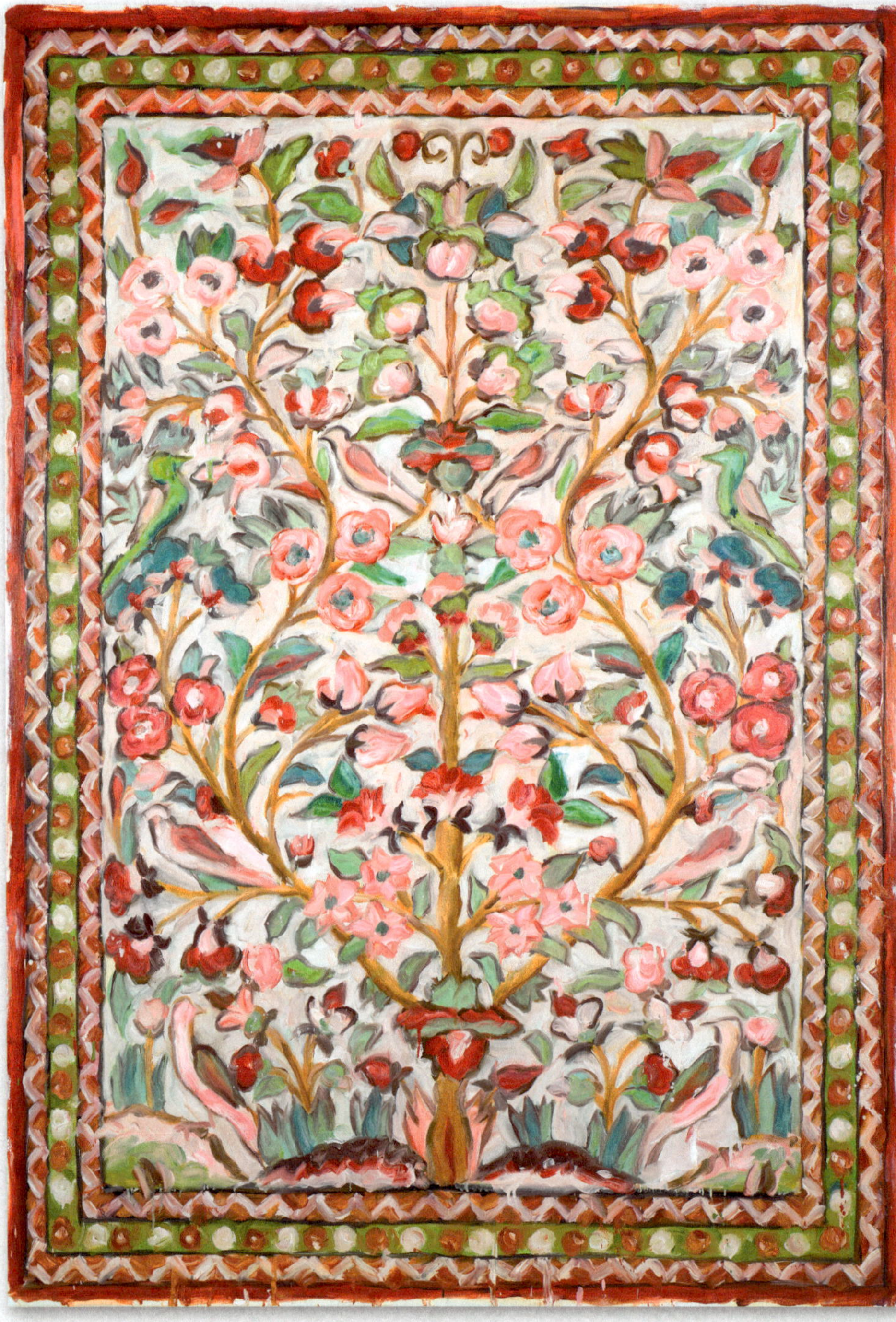

**Gebetsteppiche / *Prayer Rugs***
Öl auf Leinwand · *Oil on canvas*
195 x 140 cm · 2016

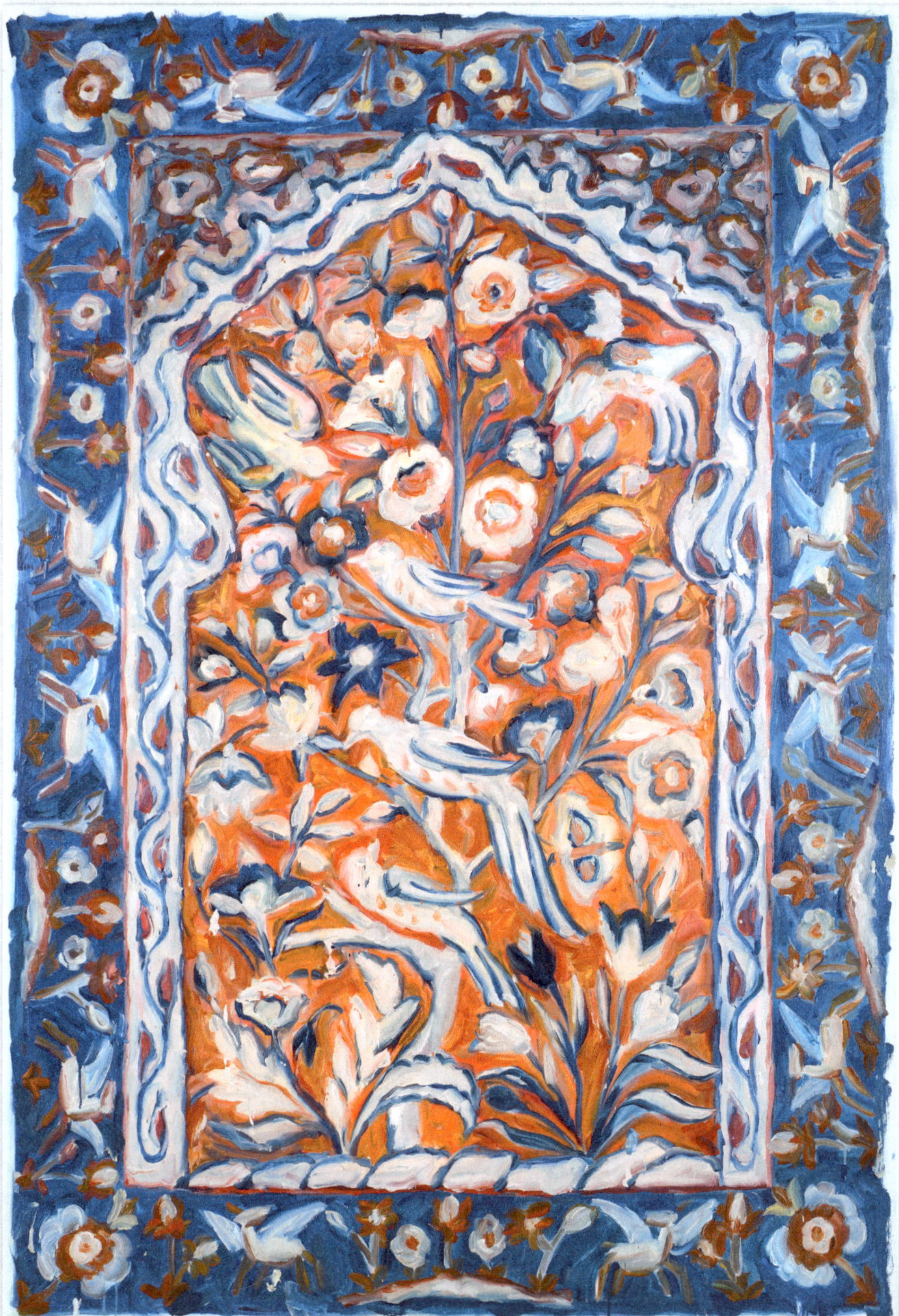

**Gebetssteppich / *Prayer Rug***
Öl auf Leinwand · *Oil on canvas*
200 x 140 cm · 2016

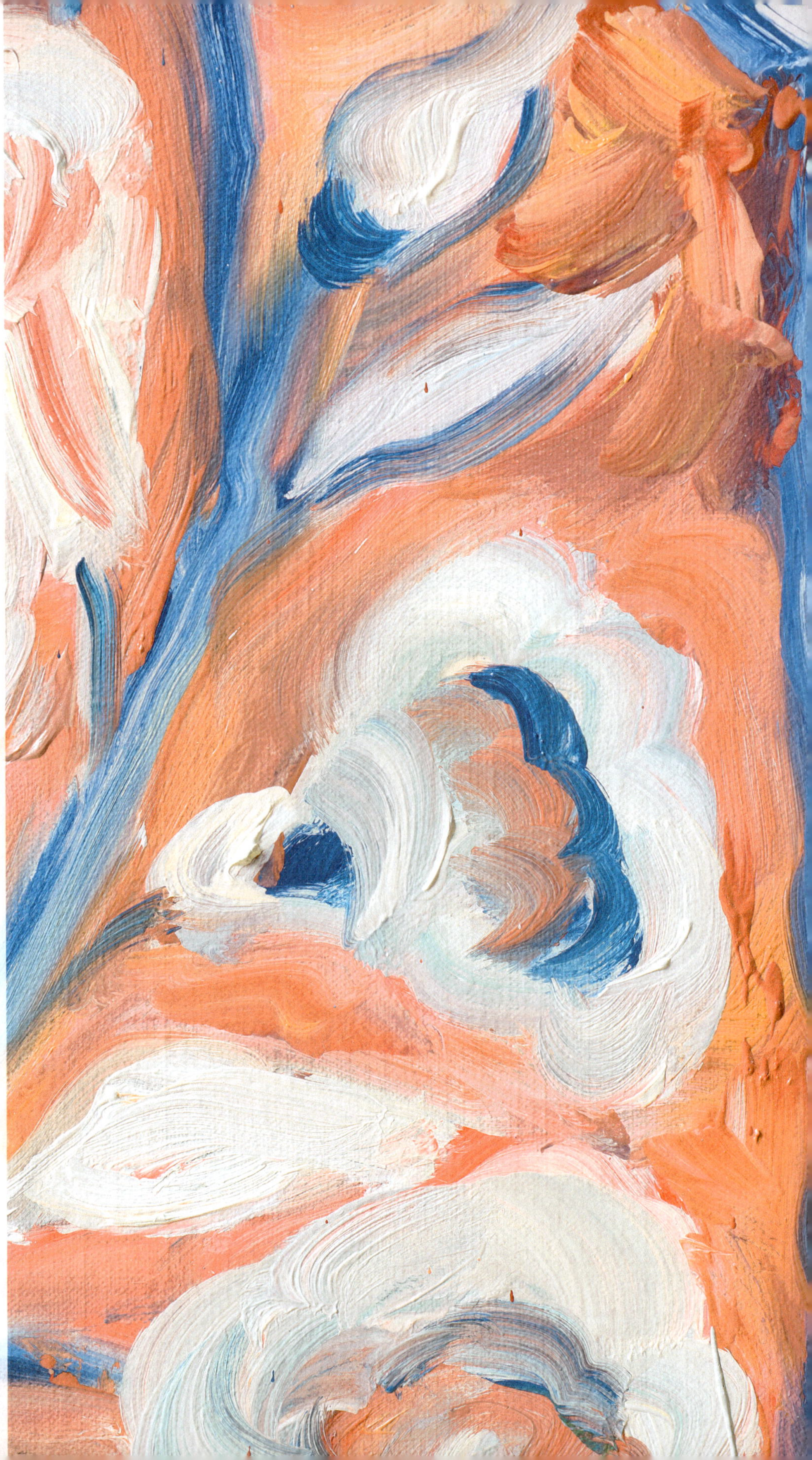

**Gebetsteppich** / ***Prayer Rug***
Detail in Originalgröße / *detail in original size*

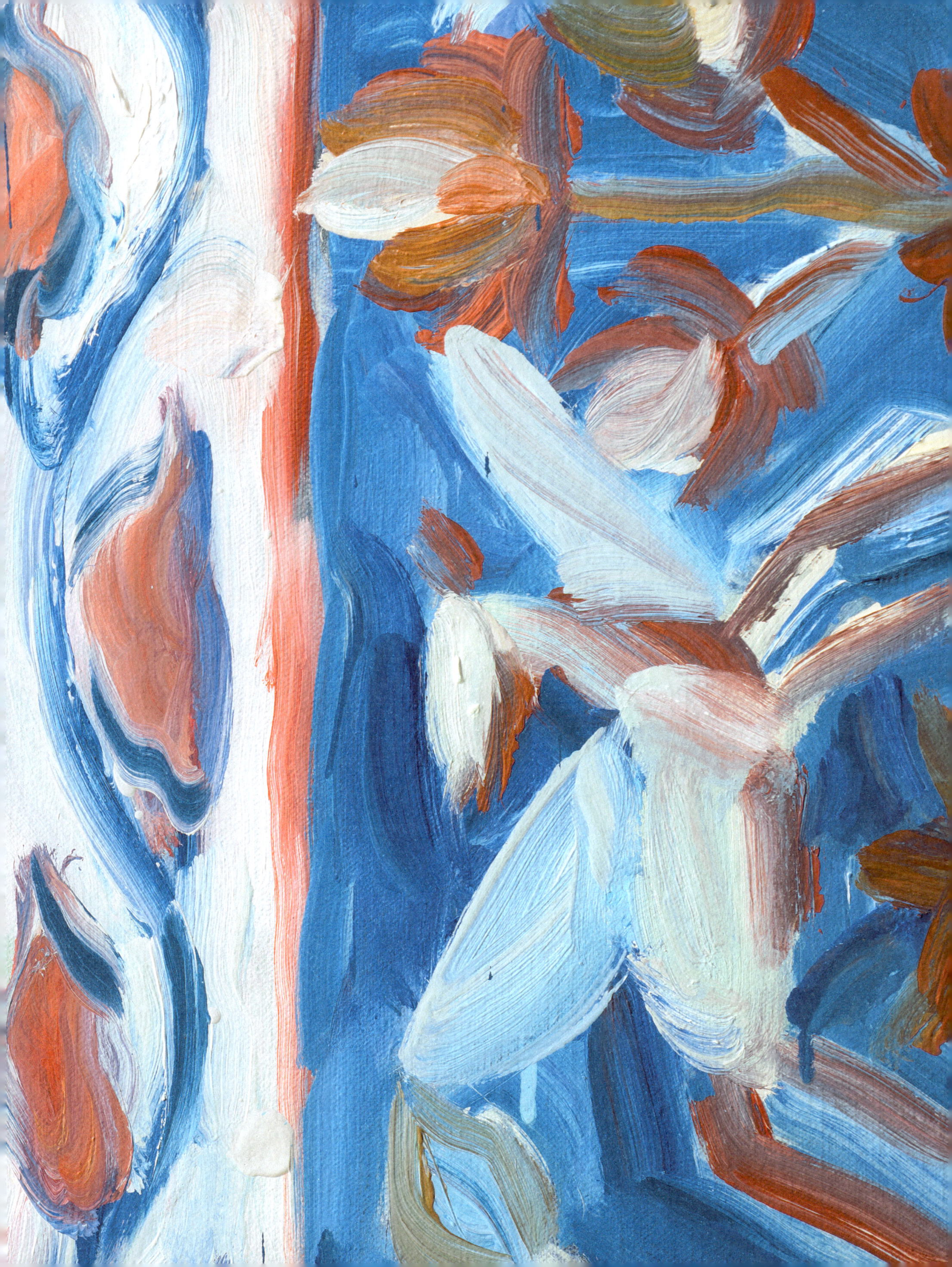

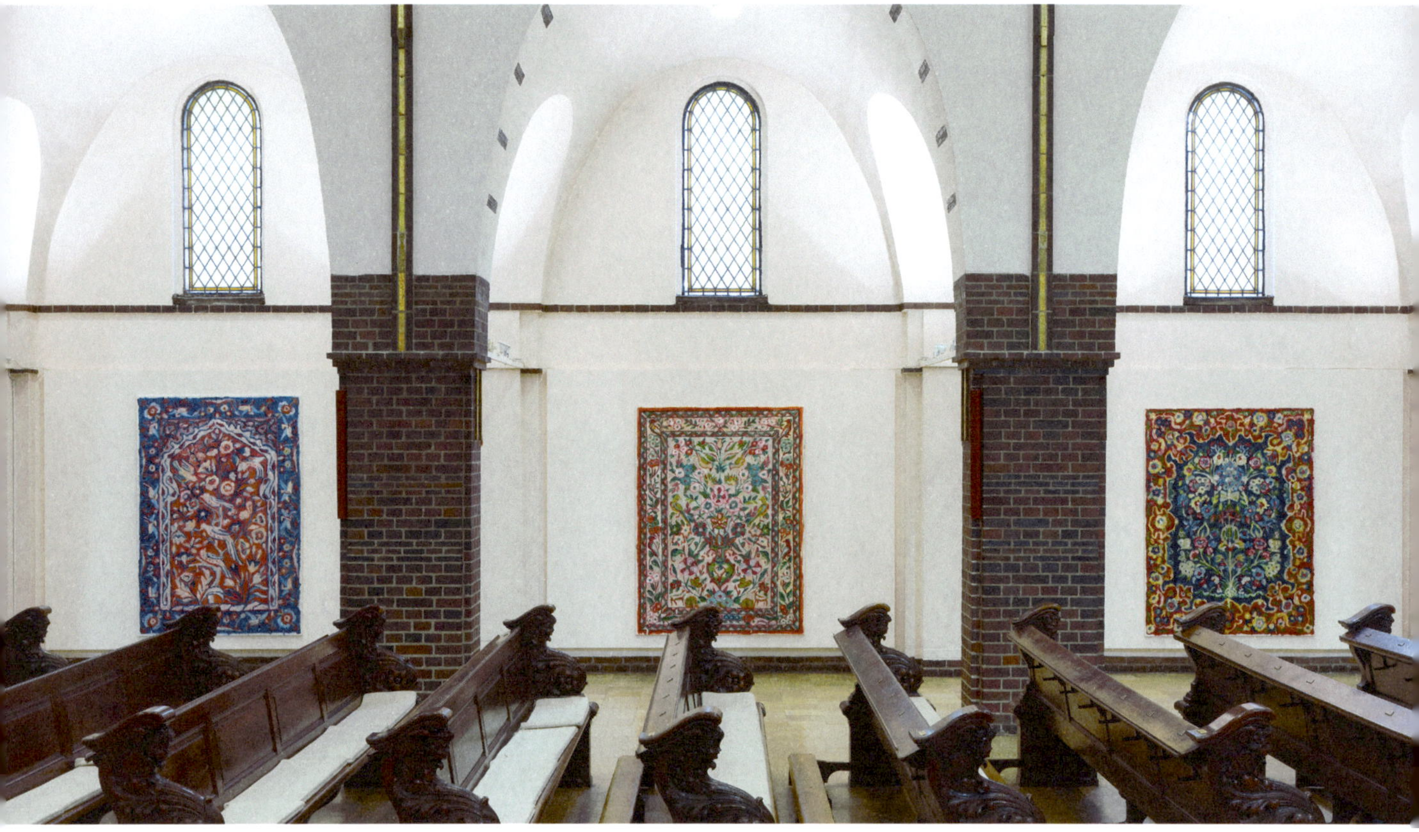

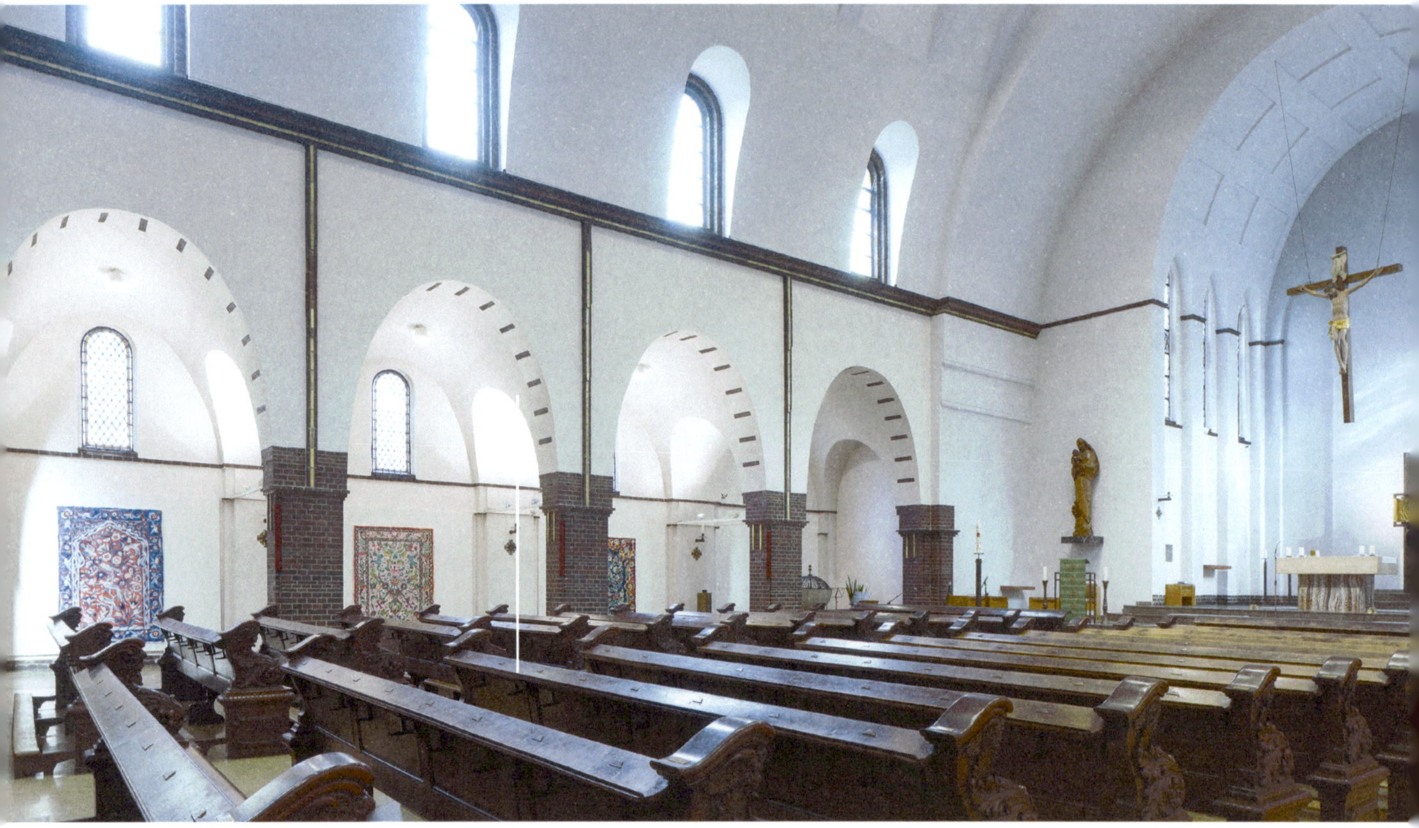

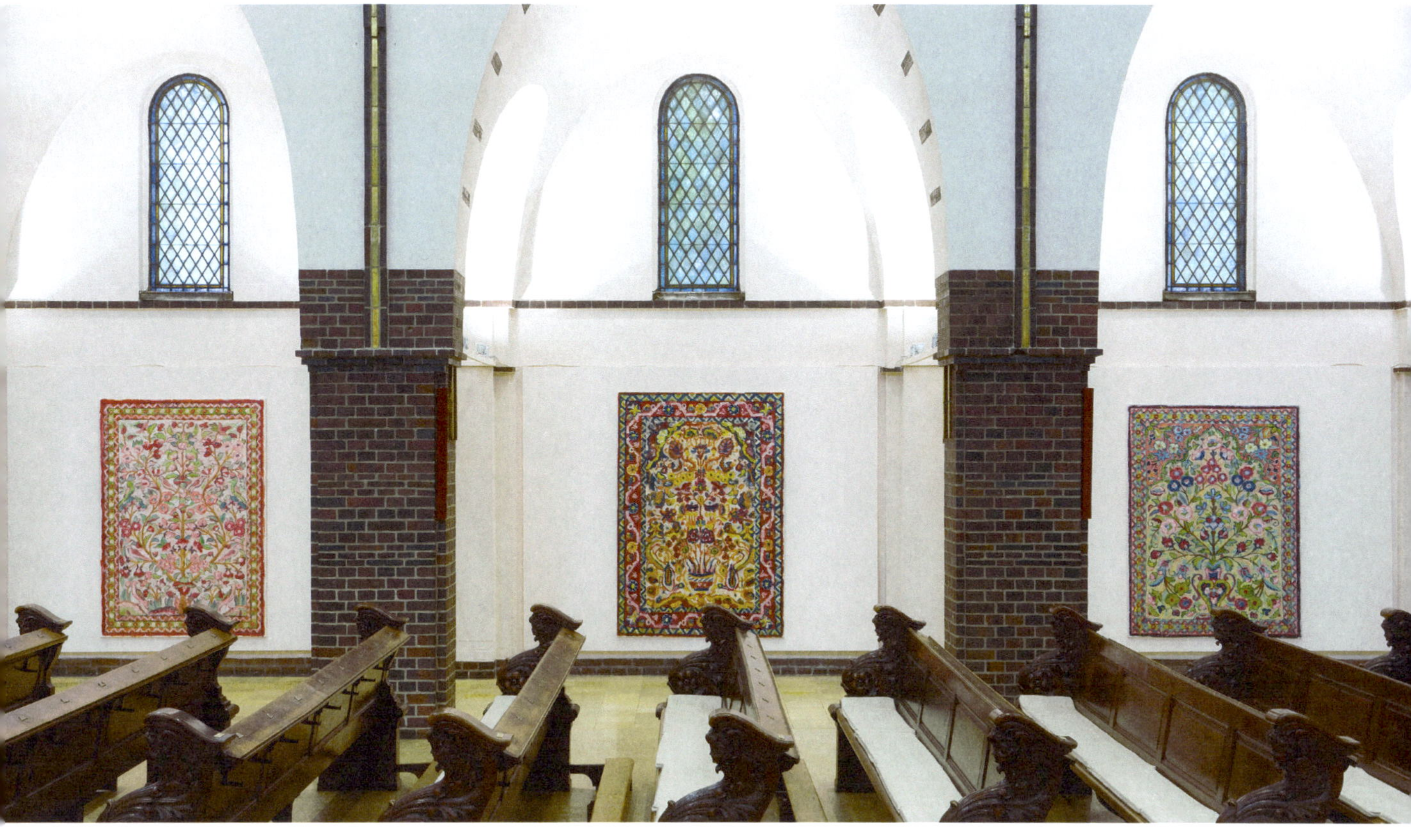

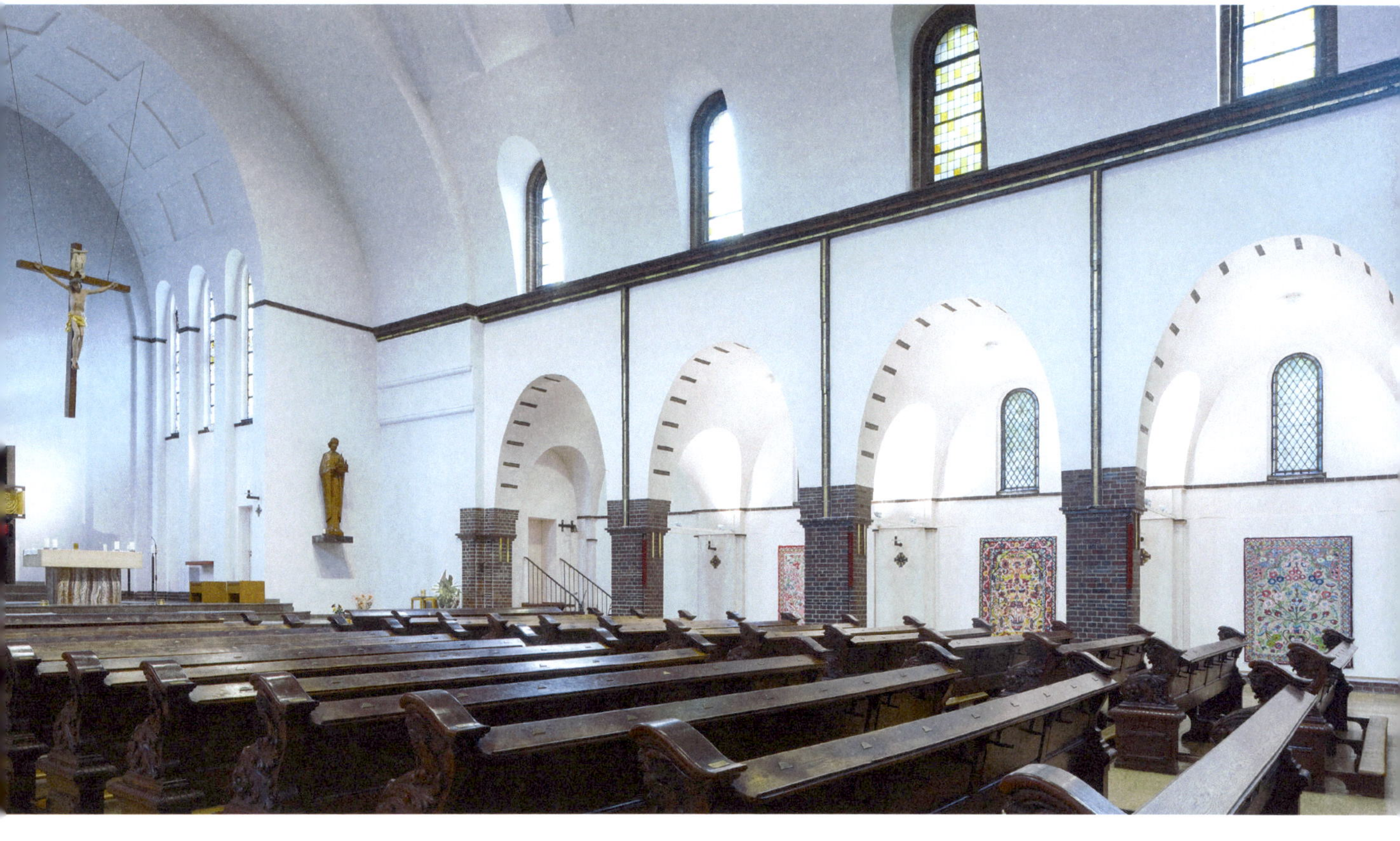

ebetsteppiche«, St. Christophorus Berlin Neukölln, Ausstellungsansicht / *»Prayer Rugs«, St. Christophorus Berlin Neukölln, Exhibition view*

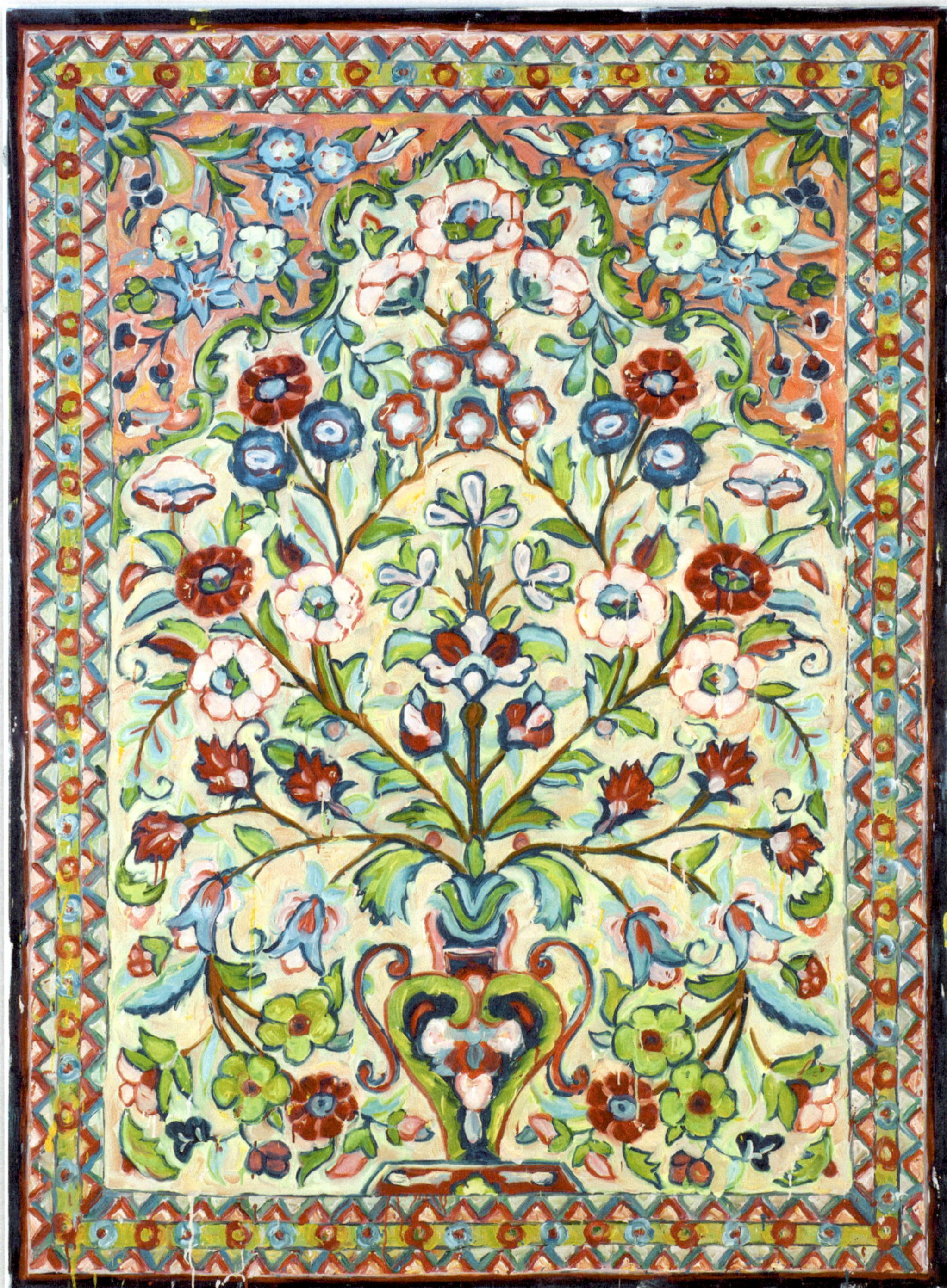

**Gebetsteppiche** / ***Prayer Rugs***
Öl auf Leinwand / *Oil on canvas*
200 x 150 cm · 2013

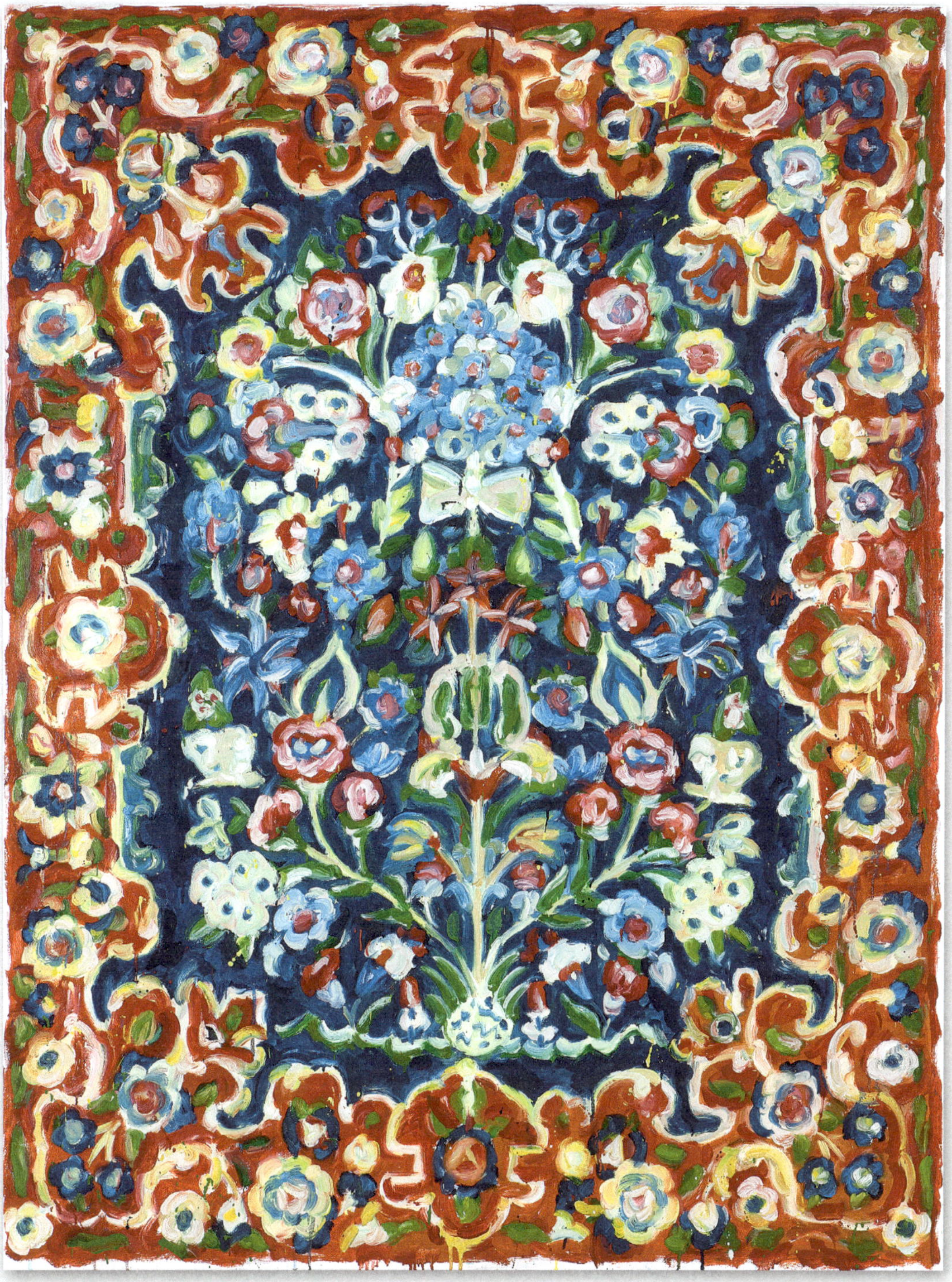

**Gebetsteppich / *Prayer Rug***
Öl auf Leinwand · *Oil on canvas*
200 x 150 cm · 2013

**Landschaft mit Bergen** / ***Landscape with mountains***
Plexiglass / *Plexiglass* · 100 x 125 cm
Öl auf Leinwand / *Oil on canvas* · 10 x 15 cm · 2014

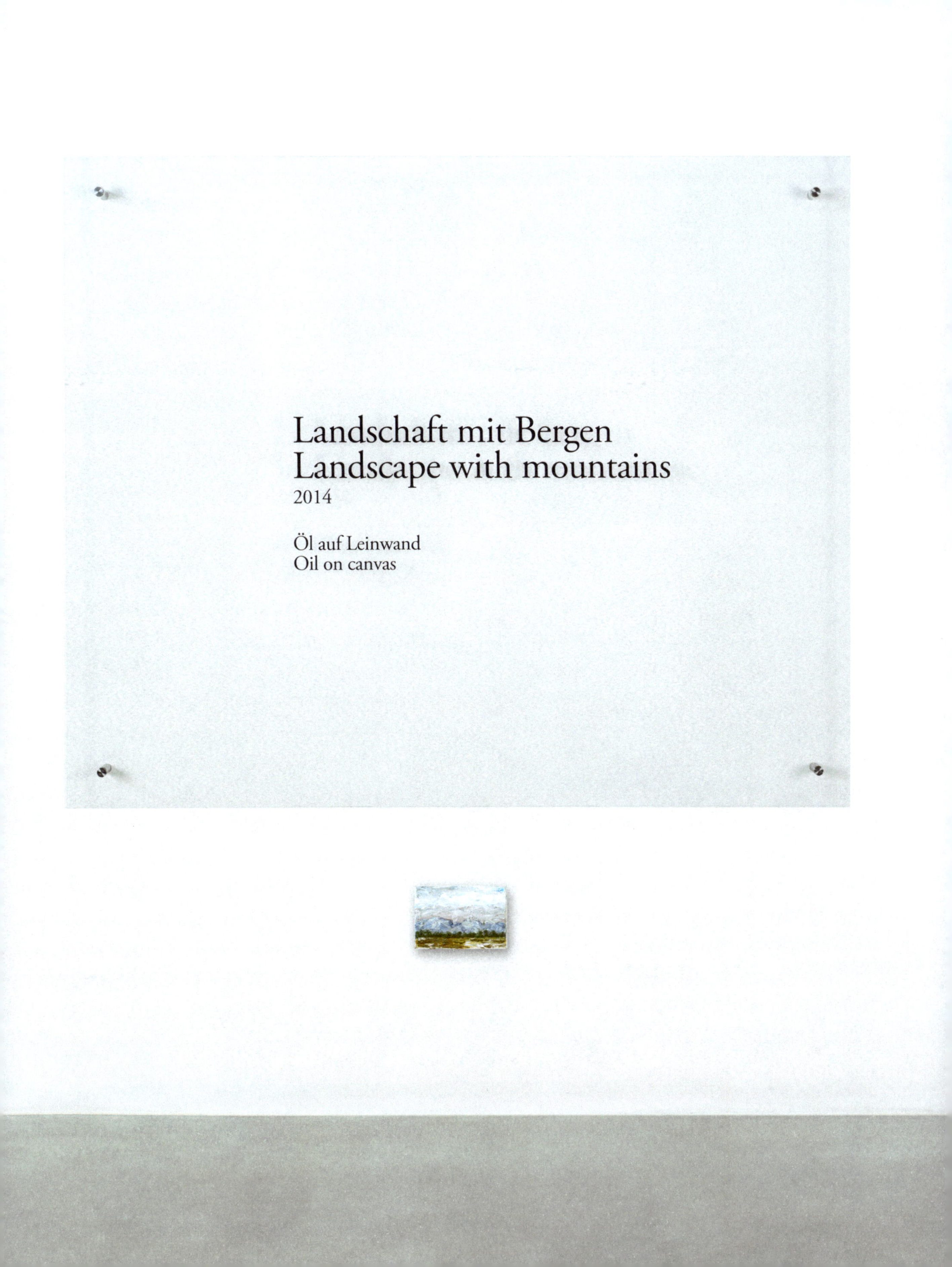
Landschaft mit Bergen
Landscape with mountains
2014
Öl auf Leinwand
Oil on canvas

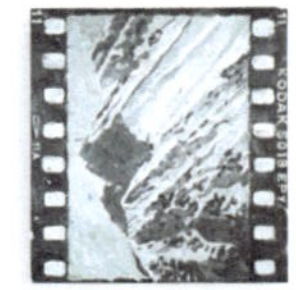

**Diafilmbild**
*Positive film picture*
135 x 150 cm
1992
S. 9

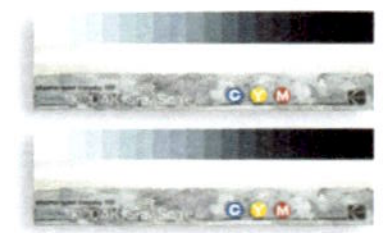

**Selfcontrol Gray**
je Tafel / *per panel*
180 x 54 cm · 1991
S. 11

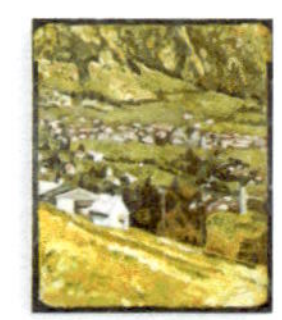

**Kodakplanfilm**
***Kodak sheet film***
126,5 x 160 cm
1992
S. 15

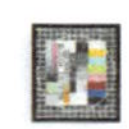

**Testbild**
*Test picture*
47 x 55 cm
1992
S. 17

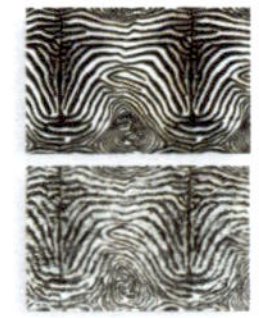

**Kunstfellimitat**
*Faux fur imitation*
2 Tafeln je / *2 panels each*
119 x 80 cm · 1987
S. 28/29

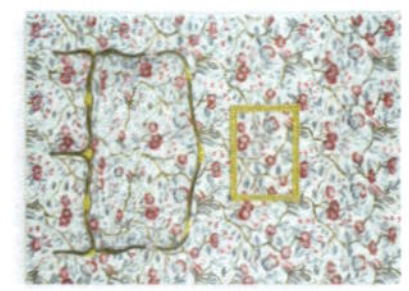

**Der Sammler**
***The collector***
200 x 150 cm · 2012
S. 31

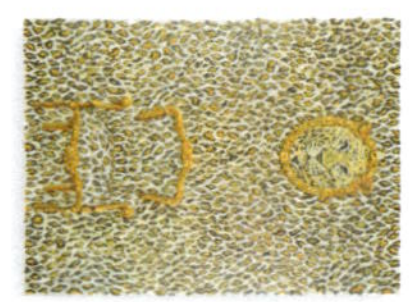

**Der Salonlöwe**
***The lounge lizard***
200 x 150 cm · 2013
S. 35

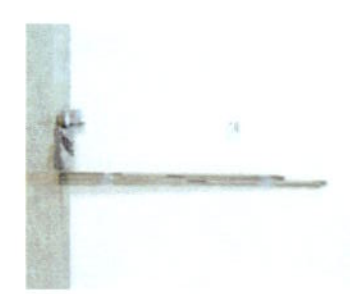

**unvollendet / *unfinished***
140 x 50 cm · 2014
S. 37

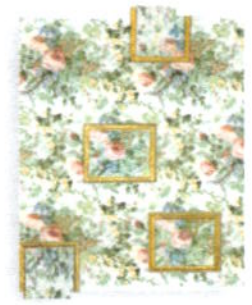

**Blumentapetenbild**
***Floral wallpaper picture***
120 x 159 cm · 2013 / 2017
S. 46/47

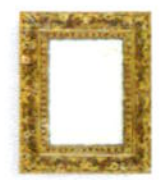

**Rahmenbild**
***Frame picture***
70 x 90 cm
2013
S. 51

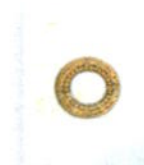

**Rahmenbild**
***Frame picture***
70 x 100 cm
2013
S. 53

**Rahmenbild**
***Frame picture***
120 x 120 cm
2012

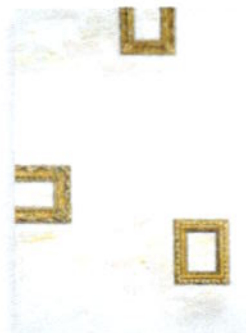

**Rahmenbild**
***Frame picture***
130 x 180 cm · 2013
S. 72/73

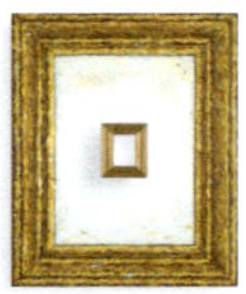

**Rahmenbild**
***Frame picture***
120 x 150 cm
2013
S. 75

**Rahmenbild**
***Frame picture***
60 x 80 cm · 2015
S. 77

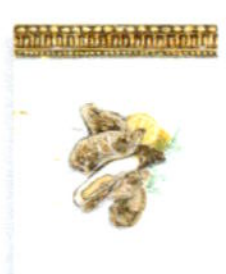

**Rahmenbild mit Austern**
***Frame picture with oysters***
110 x 150,5 cm · 2016 / 2017
S. 78/79

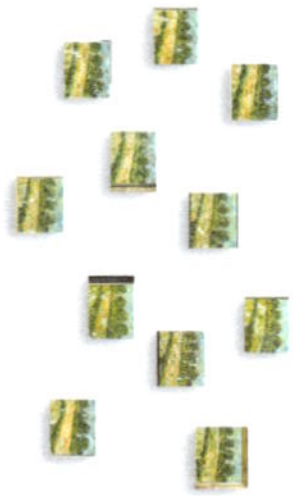

**Landschaft / *Landscape***
11 Bilder je / *11 pictures each*
24 x 30 cm · 2013 S. 92/93

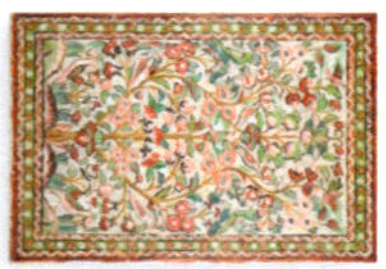

**Gebetsteppich**
***Prayer Rug***
195 x 140 cm · 2016
S. 94

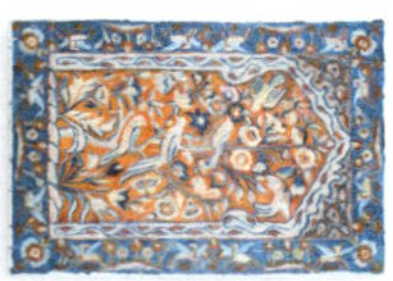

**Gebetsteppich**
***Prayer Rug***
200 x 140 cm · 2016
S. 95

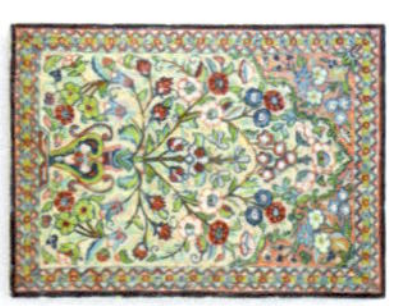

**Gebetsteppich**
***Prayer Rug***
200 x 150 cm · 2013
S. 100

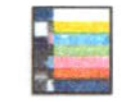

**Testbild**
*Test picture*
42,8 x 48,8 cm
1992
S. 19

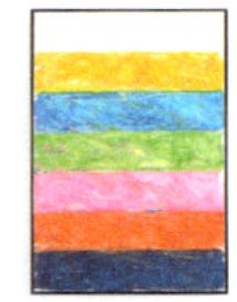

**Testbild**
*Test picture*
103,5 x 153,3 cm
2017
S. 20/21



**White noise**
81 x 80 cm · 2017
S. 23

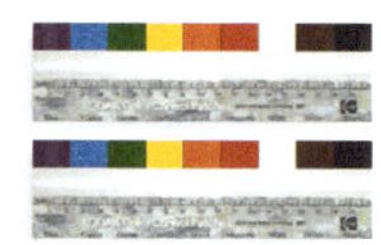

**Selfcontrol Color**
je Tafel / *per panel*
180 x 54 cm · 1991
S. 25

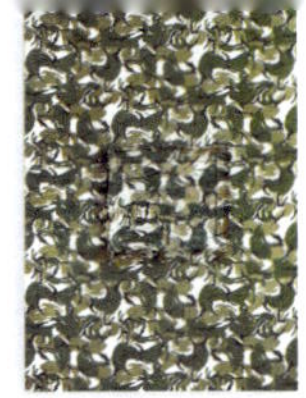

**Tarnbild**
*Camouflage picture*
145 x 210 cm · 2012
S. 38/39

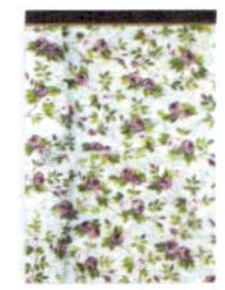

**Blumenvasenbild**
*Flower vase picture*
100 x 148 cm · 2013
S. 41

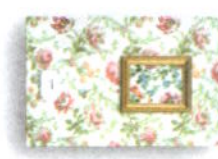

**vorBilder**
*Role models*
100 x 70 cm · 2005
S. 43

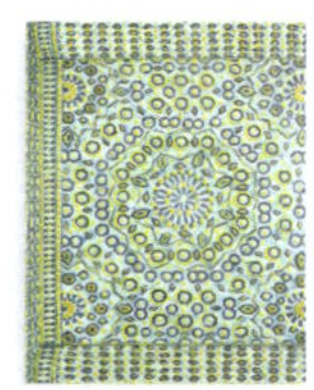

**Orientierung**
*Orientation*
150 x 200 cm · 2012
S. 44/45

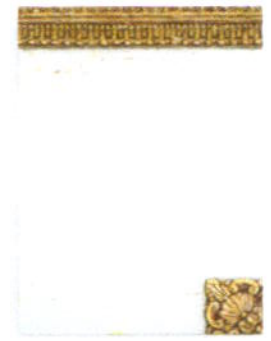

**Rahmenbild**
*Frame picture*
130 x 180 cm · 2013
S. 56/57

**Findling**
*Foundling*
13 x 10 cm
2017
S. 67

**Rahmenbild / *Frame picture***
180 x 145 cm · 2015 / 2017
S. 69

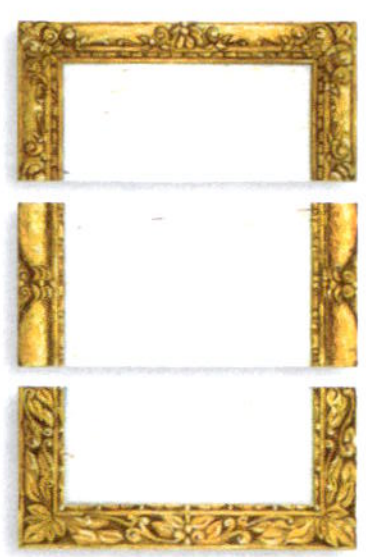

**Rahmenbild / *Frame picture***
je / *each* 180 x 90 cm · 2015
S. 70/71

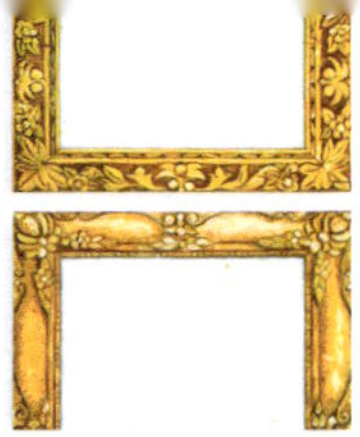

**Rahmenbild**
*Frame picture*
je / *each* 180 x 120 cm
2015
S. 80/81

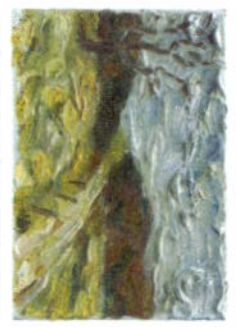

**Landschaft mit Weg**
*Landscape with path*
120 x 180 cm · 2014
S. 85

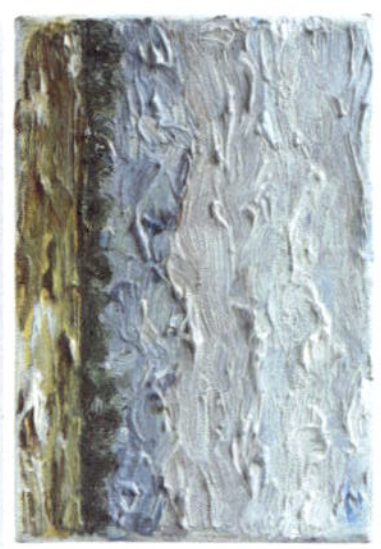

**Landschaft mit Bergen**
*Landscape with mountains*
200 x 300 cm · 2014
S. 88/89

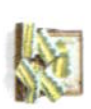

**Die Büchse der Pandora**
*Pandora's Box*
19,5 x 34 cm · 2018
S. 91

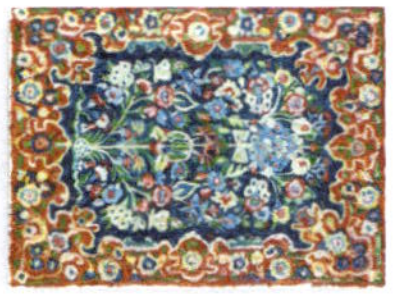

**Gebetsteppich**
*Prayer Rug*
200 x 150 cm · 2013
S. 101

**Landschaft mit Bergen**
*Landscape with mountains*
100 x 125 cm · 10 x 15 cm
2014
S. 103

**Einzelausstellungen**

2016 »Gebetsteppiche«, St. Christophorus, Berlin Neukölln
»Ein Bild ist kein Bild ist ein Bild«, Galerie Z, Berlin

2014 » vorWand und entTäuschung«, Bilder, Mannheimer Kunstverein
»Der Antifaschistische Schutzwall – oder wie ich lernte die Mauer zu lieben«, Fotoinstallation, Mannheimer Kunstverein
»Du sollst dir kein Bild machen«, Artspace POT 72 Berlin

2010 »Das Ornament der Masse«, BMW Niederlassung Mannheim

2009 Galerie Artgerecht, Eberbach
»sportlich : gesehen«, DOSB Deutscher Olympischer Sportbund, Frankfurt

1990 Galerie Michael Schulz, Berlin

1988 Studiogalerie der Kunsthalle Nürnberg

1987 Galerie Zero, Kiel
Galerie im Wasserturm, Mölln
Galerie B., Berlin

**Gruppenausstellungen**

2018 »Geld-Wahn-Sinn«, Sammlung Haupt, Reinbeckhallen, Berlin

2017 »30 Silberlinge – Kunst & Geld«, Sammlung Haupt, Mannheimer Kunstverein

2016 »Sein.Antlitz.Körper.«, St. Pius, Berlin Friedrichshain

2015 »Der Dollar leuchtet – Kunst und Zahlungsmittel«, Sammlung Haupt, Verband Deutscher Bürgschaftsbanken, Berlin
»Proud Collector«, The Grand Berlin

2013 »Money Works – Kunst mit Geld«, Sammlung Haupt, Whiteconcepts Berlin

2009 »Schauplätze – 20 Jahre Berlin im Wandel«, Wanderausstellung in Berlin

2005 »vorBilder«, Kunstverein Schwetzingen

1994 »Die Mauer«, Abgeordnetenhaus von Berlin, eine Ausstellung des Museum Haus am Checkpoint Charlie

1992 Art Basel, Edition, Basel, Galerie Michael Schulz

1991 Fiac Edition Saga, Paris, Galerie Michael Schulz

1988 »Stadtbeschreibung«, Studiogalerie der Sparkasse der Stadt Berlin West

***Solo exhibitions***

*2016 »Gebetsteppiche« (Prayer Rugs), St. Christophorus, Berlin Neukölln*
*»Ein Bild ist kein Bild ist ein Bild« (A picture is no picture is a picture),*
*Galerie Z, Berlin*

*2014 »vorWand und entTäuschung« (Pretext and disappointment),*
*Mannheimer Kunstverein*
*»Der Antifaschistische Schutzwall – oder wie ich lernte die Mauer zu lieben«*
*(The anti-fascist protective wall – or how I learned to love the wall),*
*photo installation, Mannheimer Kunstverein*
*»You shall not make for yourself an image«, Artspace POT 72 Berlin*

*2010 »Das Ornament der Masse« (The ornament of the crowd),*
*BMW Niederlassung Mannheim*

*2009 Galerie Artgerecht, Eberbach*
*»sportlich : gesehen«, DOSB Deutscher Olympischer Sportbund, Frankfurt*

*1990 Galerie Michael Schulz, Berlin*

*1988 Studiogalerie der Kunsthalle Nürnberg*

*1987 Galerie Zero, Kiel*
*Galerie im Wasserturm, Mölln*
*Galerie B., Berlin*

***Group exhibitions***

*2018 »Geld–Wahn–Sinn« (Money–Delusion–Sense), Sammlung Haupt,*
*Reinbeckhallen, Berlin*

*2017 »30 Silberlinge – Kunst & Geld« (30 Pieces of Silver – Art & Money),*
*Sammlung Haupt, Mannheimer Kunstverein*

*2016 »Sein.Antlitz.Körper.« (Being.Face.Body.), St. Pius, Berlin*

*2015 »Der Dollar leuchtet – Kunst und Zahlungsmittel«*
*(The Dollar Gleams – Art and Means of Payment), Collection Haupt,*
*Verband Deutscher Bürgschaftsbanken, Berlin*
*»Proud Collector«, The Grand Berlin*

*2013 »Money Works – Kunst mit Geld« (Money Works – Art using Money),*
*Sammlung Haupt, Whiteconcepts Berlin*

*2009 »Schauplätze – 20 Jahre Berlin im Wandel«*
*(Sites – 20 Years of Berlin Under Transformation), touring exhibition in Berlin*

*2005 »vorBilder« (Role models), Kunstverein Schwetzingen*

*1994 »The Wall«, Berlin statew parliament,*
*an exhibition of the museum house Checkpoint Charlie*

*1992 Art Basel, Edition, Basel, Galerie Michael Schulz*

*1991 Fiac Edition Saga, Paris, Galerie Michael Schulz*

*1988 »Stadtbeschreibung« (Urban Description),*
*Studiogalerie der Sparkasse der Stadt Berlin West*

**Biografie**

Armin Lindauer studierte in Düsseldorf, Konstanz und Berlin. 1984 wurde er Meisterschüler bei Prof. Helmut Lortz an der Universität der Künste Berlin (früher Hochschule der Künste). Seitdem hatte er sein Atelier in Berlin, seit 2002 in Mannheim. Von 1984 bis 1997 nimmt er verschiedene Lehrtätigkeiten an der Universität der Künste Berlin wahr. Seit 2000 ist er Professor an der Hochschule Mannheim. Seine Arbeiten werden regelmäßig ausgestellt, unter anderem in der Kunsthalle Nürnberg, in Berliner Galerien, dem Abgeordnetenhaus von Berlin, dem Kunstverein Schwetzigen sowie dem Kunstverein Mannheim. Bereits 1987 erhält er den Kunstförderpreis »Stadtzeichner von Nürnberg«. Seine angewandten Arbeiten sind in den Bereichen Buch-, Katalog- und Plakatgestaltung angesiedelt und wurden mit zahlreichen nationalen und internationalen Preisen ausgezeichnet.

**Publikationen**

2015 »Experimentelle Gestaltung – Visuelle Methode und systematisches Spiel«, mit Betina Müller, Niggli Verlag, Zürich, Schweiz

2009 »Die Berliner Mauer – Der Anfang vom Ende«, Edition Panorama, Mannheim

2007 »Die Berliner Mauer mit Daten und Fakten«, 2. erweiterte Auflage Projektagentur Bien und Giersch, Berlin

2005 »Helmut Lortz – leicht sinnig«, Verlag Hermann Schmidt Mainz

2003 »Helmut Lortz | Denkzettel«, Verlag Hermann Schmidt Mainz

2001 »Die Berliner Mauer mit Daten und Fakten«, Projektagentur Bien und Giersch, Berlin

1999 »Rund um Berlin«, 2. geänderte Auflage, Verlag Haus am Checkpoint Charlie, Berlin

1994 »Rund um Berlin«, Verlag Haus am Checkpoint Charlie, Berlin

***Biography***

*Armin Lindauer studied in Düsseldorf, Konstanz and Berlin. In 1984 he became a master-class student under Prof. Helmut Lortz at the Berlin University of the Arts (formerly Hochschule der Künste). Subsequent to that he had his studio in Berlin; it has been located in Mannheim since 2002. From 1984 until 1997 he assumed various teaching roles at the Berlin University of the Arts. He has been Professor at the University of Mannheim since 2000. His works are exhibited regularly, including at Kunsthalle Nürnberg, at Berlin galleries, the Berlin state parliament, Kunstverein Schwetzigen and Kunstverein Mannheim. He received the »Stadtzeichner von Nürnberg« (Draftsman of the city of Nuremberg) art advancement award as early as 1987. His applied works are located in the fields of book, catalogue and poster design and have been distinguished with numerous national and international awards.*

***Publications***

*2015 »Experimental Design – Visual Methods and Systematic Play«, with Betina Müller, Niggli Verlag, Zürich, Switzerland*

*2009 »Die Berliner Mauer – Der Anfang vom Ende« (The Berlin Wall – The beginning of the end), Edition Panorama, Mannheim*

*2007 »The Berlin Wall with dates and figures«, 2nd extended edition, Projektagentur Bien und Giersch, Berlin*

*2005 »Helmut Lortz – leicht sinnig« (light headed), Verlag Hermann Schmidt Mainz*

*2003 »Helmut Lortz / Denkzettel« (One in the eye), Verlag Hermann Schmidt Mainz*

*2001 »The Berlin Wall with dates and figures«, Projektagentur Bien und Giersch, Berlin*

*1997 »Rund um Berlin« (Around Berlin), 2nd modified edition, Verlag Haus am Checkpoint Charlie, Berlin*

*1994 »Rund um Berlin« (Around Berlin), Verlag Haus am Checkpoint Charlie, Berlin*

Herausgeber / *Editor*
**Martin Stather**

Konzept / *Concept*
**Armin Lindauer**

Gestaltung / *Design*
**Armin Lindauer**
**Nadine Zimmer**

Satz / *Typesetting*
**Nadine Zimmer**

Texte / *Texts*
**Thomas Friedrich**
**Martin Stather**

Übersetzung / *Translation*
**Alexandra Cox**

Fotografie / *Photography*
**Armin Lindauer**
**Marek Slipek**
**Marcus Schneider**
(Seite / *page* 82/83, 98/99)

Projektmanagement
*Project management*
**Kerber Verlag,**
**Christine Marth**

Druck / *Printing*
**NINO Druck,**
**Neustadt Weinstraße**

Bindung / *Binding*
**Großbuchbinderei Spinner,**
**Ottersweier**

Papier / *Paper*
**Soporset, 110 g / *110 g/sqm***
**Soporset, 300 g / *300 g/sqm***

Die Deutsche Nationalbibliothek verzeichnet diese Publikation in der Deutschen Nationalbibliografie; detaillierte bibliografische Daten sind im Internet über http://dnb.dnb.de abrufbar. / *The Deutsche Nationalbibliothek lists this publication in the Deutsche Nationalbibliografie; detailed bibliographic data are available on the Internet at http://dnb.dnb.de.*

Vertrieb / *Published by*
Kerber Verlag, Bielefeld
Windelsbleicher Str. 166–170
33659 Bielefeld
Germany
Tel +49 (0) 5 21/9 50 08-10
Fax +49 (0) 5 21/9 50 08-88
info@kerberverlag.com

*Kerber, US Distribution*
*ARTBOOK | D.A.P.*
*75 Broad Street, Suite 630*
*New York, NY 10004*
*Tel +1 (212) 627-1999*
*Fax +1 (212) 627-9484*

Kerber-Publikationen werden weltweit in führenden Buchhandlungen und Museumsshops angeboten (Vertrieb in Europa, Asien, Nord- und Südamerika). / *Kerber publications are available in selected bookstores and museum shops worldwide (distributed in Europe, Asia, South and North America).*



ISBN 978-3-7356-0523-8
www.kerberverlag.com

Printed in Germany